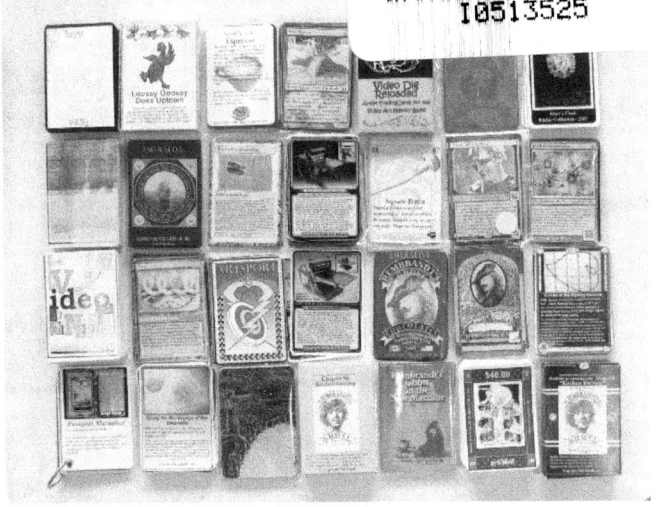

ACTC:

Artist's Collectible Trading Cards

By Bill H. Ritchie

First draft of a catalog raisonné of Bill Ritchie's Artist's Collectible Trading Cards made between 1995 and 2015 as sketches for works of art, CTC games, and strategic plans for his artist's assets and legacy transfer.

Artists Collectible Trading Cards

Contents

Foreword 4

1 Poster Deck - 1998 10

2 Loosey Goosey Does Uptown 14

3 Blue Saucer 21

4 Wavey Square Buried at Bush School 24

5 Video Dig Reloaded 27

6 Copper Plates 32

7 Artist's Clock 37

8 SPEACON Deck 40

9 Emeralda cards 44

10 Emeralda Dreaming 48

11 Galleon Halfwood Press 53

12 Printmaker Genius Sample 56

13 Sam Hamrick 59

14 Pepin-Etcher/astronomer 62

15 Video 'N Print 65

16 Kite with Leaves 68

17 ArtsPort Resident Genius 70

18 Mini Halfwood Press 73

19 Rembrandt's Ghost Chocolates 75

20 Rembrandt's Amsterdam 80

21 Screen of the Rolling Sorcerer 84

22 Passport Metaphor 87
23 Study for the Voyage of the Emeralda 90
24 Cyanotype Poster Cut-up 92
25 Kitchen Etching 95
26 Rembrandt's Ghost Covers 98
27 Emeralda Games 100
28 Printopolis 107
29 Conclusion 112

Artists Collectible Trading Cards

Foreword

Until I invented the idea, I don't think there had been an effort to use collectible trading cards as a means of *artist's asset management and legacy transfer*. It's my invention for my family, friends (patrons) and the worldwide community of printmaking practitioners. This book is my way of documenting my experiments toward the invention of Artists Collectible Trading Card Games (ATCG).

The potential of collectible trading card games for artist's asset management and legacy transfer strategies first occurred to me in the early 1990's when I learned about *Magic: The Gathering.* MTG, invented by Richard Garfield after Peter Adkison's suggestion. It was an immediate success and gained a high profile in the collectible card genre. I was so enamored by the idea that I made a diptych, posing as the inventor of a successful kind of collectible card game.

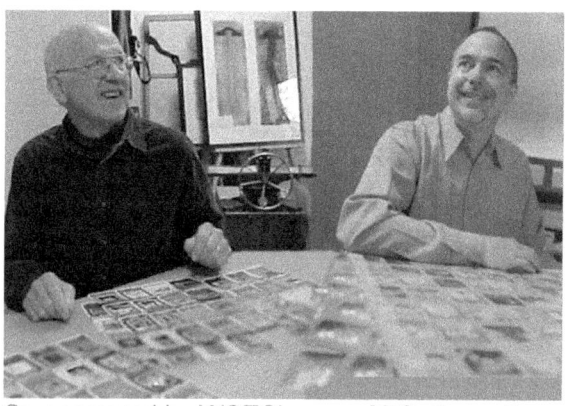

So enamored by WOTC' game, MtG, the author pasted his image alongside Peter Adkison's in a photo.

Because I am not remotely interested in games as pure recreation or gambling, the purpose of MTG was obscure at first. The producer, *Wizards of the Coast,* hired artists to make the images on the cards, and it was this that got my attention. These put food on artists' tables (or so I thought) and that was a good thing—and would be even better if printmakers got in on this new source of income.

As I am always reminded of how paying work is needed by artists. My days as a college art teacher saw the need for incorporating economic planning for artists and their families. Although I landed a college teaching job and lifetime tenure, I knew that most of my students would not be as lucky. They'd have to make it on their own if they wanted to make a life in the arts.

Among other resources, the part time work of illustrating collectible cards seemed to me like a good thing for independent artists. Not only illustrating for blockbuster games like MTG, but for the many companies that needed tech-savvy artists. Commercial collectible trading card game producers might even consider a royalty scheme, or so I was thinking in those days.

Or, if artists made collectible cards independently as works of art, these artist's cards might be better still. Trading cards have characteristics that are a little like artist's stamps. Stamps by my friend the Seattle artist C. T. Chew, for example, became an art genre and he sold them in art galleries and, at the time of this writing shares in the worldwide mail art community.

Artists Collectible Trading Cards

As I wanted more than what commercial publishers offer, I conceived of collectible cards or decks of cards that are authentic works of art in their own right—outside of mainstream commercial trading cards. A deck has the potential to be more than meets the eye. It can be a vehicle for expression with a scope for fiction. A deck might even have potential as a method of artists' asset management and legacy transfer.

As an over-arching background to all this speculation is my life-game, *Emeralda: Games for the gifts of life*. It is more a philosophy than, by definition, a game. One woman, Florence Scoville Shinn, wrote a book titled, *How to Play the Game of Life*, and I took to heart her advice. She was of the late 19th Century idealist movement with Emerson and Thoreau, advising that we tap into the unknowable and weave a fabric of our life plan for ourselves, for those we love, and for our community.

Weaving one's life game might overflow the boundaries of our existence, pass beyond the borders of our country and be useful to great numbers of others. This great notion is what keeps some artists toiling at their art and craft—providing motivation to overcome indifference and setbacks that a consumer society usually hands us.

Confucius advised, *Better to play games than do nothing at all*. With the rise of video games we have come to a time when video games can be works of art. The software for a video game is not the fruit of only one person's mind and he or she is not thinking about life plans the way artists may, and artists who work on the games are relegated to peonage work like the slaves that build the pyramids for the Pharaohs.

Richard Garfield didn't invent MTG working by himself. As boy, long before MTG, he was collaborating with other people because that's how games like *Dungeons and Dragons* worked. Garfield's first cards were hand-drawn, then he made them on office copiers.

By nature, games are social and it is here where I find a similarity between printmaking and collectible trading card games: Printmaking is social, too, almost game-like.

Making printing plates, inking and preparing the sundry items that go with them (paper-making, skills with tools, etc.) are closer to performance than the arts to which art schools usually associate printmaking, i.e., painting and drawing.

When I was at the UW, experiments by the students in my printmaking and video art classes demonstrated that being time-based, printmaking is like music and theater, and therefore printmaking rightfully shares with performance arts—closer to these than with painting and drawing.

In making a printing plate, artists compose a score, like writing the writing of a musical score, a stage or screen play. Performing this "score" requires lot of practice and then it needs an instrument, such as a printing press, a wooden spoon, a baren, or squeegee. Often this performance requires the help of other people besides the one who claims the artistic role.

What results from their collective performance is not only important as a work of art. It is an artifact of a happening, a moment that remains long after this *time-based* and repeatable performance. Printmaking becomes the experiences that we seek. The rewards lie in the challenges to the skills and fun of making plates and printing them and, often, in the company of others.

The art of printmaking has been associated with card games for a long, long time. When printing techniques were developed well enough, printed cards for all kinds of entertainment took the place of most of the hand-drawn and painted cards. In recent times, artist's trading cards came into vogue and they represent a spectrum of variations, from handmade cards, low-relief sculpture, stamping, scrapbooking and digital prints.

In matters of artist-designed games, mine addresses the eternal dilemma of the creative, innovative artist. I started about the time that I left the security of university teaching in the mid-1980s. The challenge was, (1) how to sell art without selling out, (2) how to cope with being an artist in Seattle in this scientific and technology age and (3) how to live life virtuously and virtually on the threshold of human species' destruction of Earth's human life sustainability.

Now, in 2015, at the age I am (mid-seventies) what else is there to do but catalog and evaluate what I achieved in an interesting way? This book may be a useful accounting of one my projects—*Artists Collectible Trading Card Games*. As I write this book, in a corner of my imagination I wonder, what a publisher of mass-produced books will ask.

Would it sell? How much promotion would it take? The answer comes from a small voice, echoing from another corner: *"Mass production? How 19th Century! Wake up—it's the 21st Century!"*

On my own, among my social media following or those who own works of art and design I made, I speculate:

Could a crowd-funding project turn this book, a catalog of my card experiments, into something better?

Who knows? The cards and this book about my cards is in keeping with my philosophical life-game, *Emeralda*; my task is part of asset management and legacy transfer because—as you see—it is digital, conceived and do-able in the media of its own creation (referring to the first edition of this book as a Kindle ebook; a paper version may follow).

In this way I follow one of my guiding lights—Muriel Strode—who wrote, "I will not follow where the path may lead, but I will go where there is no path, and I will leave a trail," and, Confucius, "Better to play games than do nothing at all," and Jane McGonigal, "… *Games Make Us Better and … They Can Change the World."*

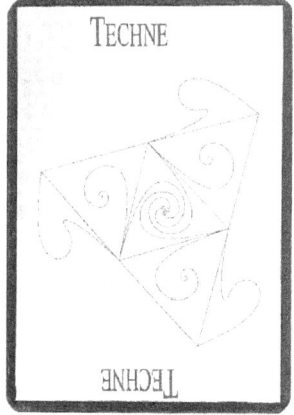 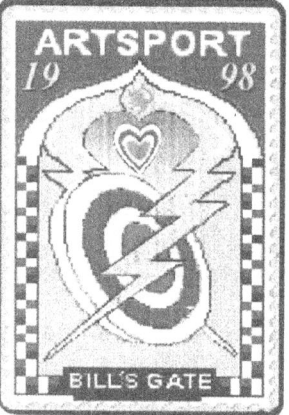

Figure 1: Two sides of a Poster Deck 1998 example card from, two sides shown. All the cards have the right image on them as the backs of the cards.

1 Poster Deck - 1998

The Poster Deck is a deck of fifty-four cards made by cutting up a *Cyanotype 1980* poster and printing or gluing the ArtsPort heraldic design or logo on the other side. (ArtsPort is one of the islands of domains-of-expertise in the Emeralda Region—more about that later.) They are edged in black.

A few have what appear to be suggestions written in freehand – or instructions for gameplay. For example, "Design floor print bin," which refers to a common piece of furniture for art galleries.

"Update, edit website home page," reads another. "Read and sort, delete, reply to email,"

"Read, correct, format P65 [PageMaker—forerunner to today's Adobe software] iteration of Gates biography," "Design system Last Love Letter to instruct on label-to-database," and "Mat, frame, curate prints."

"Update mail list database, trouble shoot," "Update Gates calendar and correct Rule," "Install art on wall," "Get a block started for next color," "Receive postcards and get bulk mail class schedule," and, "Design Emeralda Card Game (this one)."

This side of the cards has the names of the four Women-who-fell-to-Earth—Aurel (13), Media (13), Techne (13) and Tetra (13) and also Omnium Gatherum (2). This provides four suits, one for each of the women from the Emeralda Legend. Also, two Omnium Gatherum cards provides for the two brothers.

These numbers approximate the size of typical playing cards, as for Poker: An ace, numbers 2-10, Jack, Queen and King, with two Jokers. I suspect I was working on a board game when I made these cards. The purpose of the game was to teach printmaking concomitant with conventional playing card strategies.

Also on the art side is a diagram of the tetrahedron. The design was made so that a flat printed outline could be cut out of paper, folded and assembled so as to make a tetrahedron. In the

Artists Collectible Trading Cards

Emeralda legend, these tetrahedrons were the form of the spaceships which, clustered, traveled from the Planet Fleura, also known as the Flower Planet. Each craft landed in six places on planet Earth. In the legend, these immortal aliens seek to find one another. One of them, a man under the name of Omnium Gatherum, seeks to end Earth's human life sustainability. The other man and the sisters seek to stop him.

The game mechanic is unknown; only the directives on some of the cards give a hint of what I was thinking. They look like a "to do" list or a diary of the day in my life in 1998. This was the year that I made the 31-day series, *Emeralda Interviews* as another strategy to figure out the game, Emeralda and so make it playable for other people.

In all, Emeralda is a structure for artists' asset management and legacy transfer—something like a living will. By learning Emeralda, my goal is to learn the artist's way of helping family, community, country and humanity save Earth's human life sustainability.

The box

A handmade box for this deck is made of glossy gray paper stock cut from a package labeled *Instant Replay*. Inside the top flap the date is written, *980510*, which means May 10, 1998. On one side of the box I taped a paper with six statements taken from the book, *Think and Grow*

Rich, by Napoleon Hill, the volume I read which was published in 1960—the year I graduated from High School. I didn't read the book until many years later, however, when I resigned from the UW and was looking for self-help books.

When I review the six guidelines, I wonder if they helped to form my life game, *Emeralda: Games for the gifts of life*. Reading Hill's life story, you find that his claim to spiritual guides on whom he relied. He was open about these "voices in his head" and published a book about it.

It was in his more famous book, *Think and Grow Rich*, where I learned about Elmer Gates, who was among those Hill interviewed. Elmer Gates was the man after whom I named the Gates Prize which became part of the Emeralda Legend and back story for my games.

Artists Collectible Trading Cards

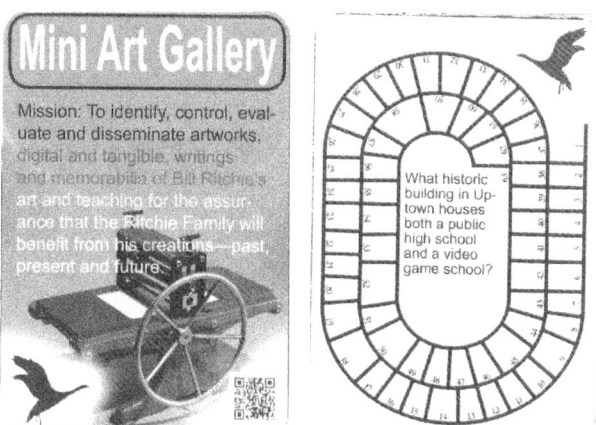

Figure 2: Two sides of a Loosey Goosey card. This one features the Ritchie family's Mini Art Gallery. Multiple cards to make up a deck, and two decks made for the Loosey Goosey tournament. 2014.

2 Loosey Goosey Does Uptown

The purpose of the game for which I designed these cards—*Loosey Goosey Does Uptown* has never been played at the time of this writing. It is a "game with purpose." Games with purpose replaced the category, *serious games* in the video game industry.

Apparently the word *serious* is a turn-off for financial speculators aiming to get rich quick in the video game industry. Like educational games and edutainment, *serious*, *educational*, *and spiritual* or other such -isms are about as welcome to capital investor meetings as a minister at a strip club.

Games with purpose other than to make cash profits are tolerable but not easily funded by these investors.

As an investor in intellectual capital I make artist's collectible trading card games (ACTCG), and this takes money and time; if it's money you need for a collectible card game, you must mortgage your house (if you have one), get friends or family to help, or—as with MTG—take your cards to the market.

They first sold decks of cards for *Magic: The Gathering*, at Seattle's Pike Place Market. If you can't get face to face with customer/players, then a crowd funder might work for you—maybe for *Loosey Goosey*, I thought.

Loosey's story

Here's why I made the Loosey Goosey cards: In 2014 I renewed my missionary zeal for a printmaking center of some kind. I had started reaching out as far back as 1980 when I was a professor at the UW. On a sabbatical I went around the world to collect proof that, as an institution in the arts and humanities, the UW needed to *Go global and green*. Our students needed new programs in safety and economics in the printmaking studios and new printing technologies.

My proof was evident, and I made my point but I lost my job in the process; so my dream of a Seattle-based, global outreach for media arts had to

Artists Collectible Trading Cards

wait forty years. Now, after thirty years, the pieces began to come together and under the name, *Northwest Print Center & Incubators*, NPC&I.

It happened that two new buildings—200 apartments and commercial space—will be built near our gallery, so I made the building block my preferred site for the NPC&I. In my conversations with one of the architects, I learned that the City might give preferred treatment to a developer who allocated space for arts and culture.

A project on Capitol Hill—an arts center famously showed up as the poster child for City and developer cooperation. Neighbors working with developers and the city to provide for arts, culture, and commerce good for everyone, including housing for people employed in the arts.

Thinking I could do the same, I upped my community activism and went to a meeting for our neighborhood, called *Uptown*. A leader of the organization—John Coney— initialized getting Uptown cultural arts district status. Mr. Coney, unfortunately, would only live a few more months, leaving the rest to a committee. I joined in because I want the *Northwest Print Center & Incubators* to locate in the new building, helping to make it a cultural asset to the neighborhood.

The art committee's kickoff for cultural arts districtification started with a bang. Planned by a charrette expert in urban planning and an urban designer, about fifty people showed up—a lively, friendly crowd of city councilors, arts commissioners and architects and representatives of all the arts organizations in Uptown and the Seattle Center (which is in Uptown, actually).

Everyone—the Seattle Opera, Pacific Northwest Ballet, several theaters, the historical society—was excited by the benefits that might come them. There a few restaurants and design studios, too; I was among the few independent artists.

It was a rousing show. Five tables were set up for mind-melding. I was with seven other people—all strangers to me—and we pored over Uptown's map, marking and tagging it with ideas. I suggested an APP for Uptown Cultural Arts. At the end, the tables tallied their priorities and the next step was called for; by cheering and clapping, a Badminton Rally was to be the most likely to succeed as the Next Big Step.

Badminton? Really? I was mystified. I didn't get it until, later, I saw that a Badminton rally had been held several times to raise money and cheer for the theater hosting this meeting—*On the Boards*. The prize was a bottle of Jim Beam.

Seriously?

Thinking I could upstage it, and mindful that I was a stranger, an independent and an outsider, I decided to invent a game that would help get

Artists Collectible Trading Cards

cultural arts districtification off the ground and into the air. *Loosey Goosey* cards, part of *Loosey Goosey Does Uptown*, resulted.

Cards and boxes

The cards are in four suits of geese posing in four attitudes—*angry, silly, passive* and *flying high*. There are 64 cards in each of the suits' decks.

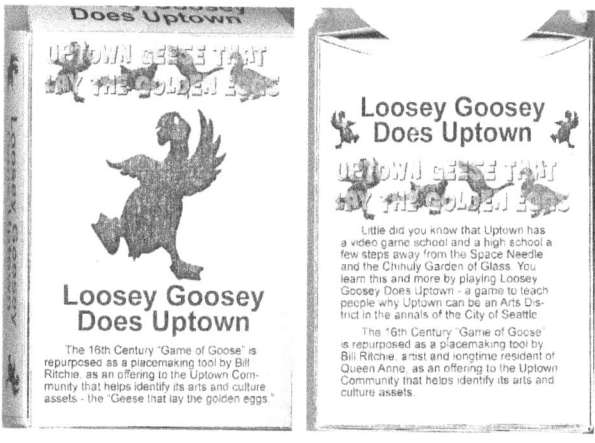

Figure. 3: Two sides of a box for 64 Loosey Goosey cards. Each suit—geese in one of four attitudes (angry, flying high, docile and silly—has its own box. One is shown here. The examples in the photos are in their sketchy, black-and-white first state.

On one side of each card are the logos, photos, mission statement, and QR code to the website of each of sixty four cultural arts assets in Queen

Anne. Printed in color, the layout and design of the card mimics typical collectible trading cards.

On the other side of each card is printed a question about the heritage or a factoid relating this cultural arts asset card to this neighborhood or Seattle in general. For example, on that of the *Queen Anne Historical Society*—a question about the historic sites or events related to Uptown would be logical. Each organization or group makes their own set of a four-card deck, and their own questions.

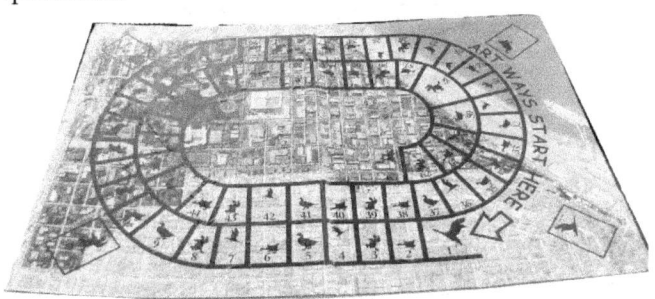

Figure 4: The Loosey Goosey tournament tabletop game board, a sketch in black and white, the cells' pathway for the game superimposed on a map of the Uptown neighborhood of Queen Anne, Seattle.

This table-top game board is patterned on the 16th Century "Game of Goose." It is somewhat like Monopoly. The tournament in which the cards are used is a social, get acquainted event and fund-raiser where two teams of eight players each try to win all the golden eggs. The golden egg metaphor

Artists Collectible Trading Cards

came from the city's arts and culture office literature which mentions what numerous US city planners know to be true: *Artists are the geese that lay the golden eggs of our city's economies.*

The prize, of course, is a gold-filled egg.

The game parts, besides the golden eggs, include dice and hardwood quarter-eggs that serve as playing pieces. At the time of this writing, there is a web site for Loosey.

Scan the QR code to link up with the development website or key in. http://tinyurl.com/o9saqam

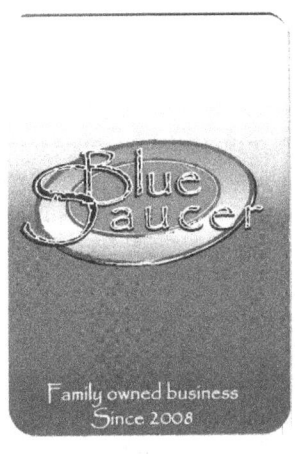

Figure 5: Blue Saucer, front and back, are cards that were to be used to build a loyal customer base at the Blue Saucer Coffee shop in Seattle.

3 Blue Saucer

One of our daughters, Billie Jane Bryan, opened a coffee shop and named it, "Blue Saucer." My wife Lynda and I were part owners. I designed Artist Collectible Trading Cards to match all the drinks Billie offered—latte, Americano, etc., and made each one a *collectible* card marketing loosely based on punch-card systems coffee shops use.

The cards were to be sold as a deck of a dozen cards, with each card being redeemable for whichever drink the card represented, i.e., its face value. The customer surrendered each card to the cashier; if the card was in new condition, this card could be recycled into another deck and resold.

Artists Collectible Trading Cards

To add incentives by making the cards collectible, customers had the option of keeping the card. In this instance the cashier was to cancel the card with a stamp and embossing (like a corporate seal). It would make the card unusable to exchange for drinks, but—stamped and embossed with the Blue Saucer coffee shop seal—it was collectible or might used otherwise, such as for promotional events, loyalty parties, trading, or games.

Thirteen Blue Saucer cards remain in the Ritchie Family Art collection. In addition to these Blue Saucer cards there are three cards are from another promotion effort in 2008.

This one was part of an Earth Day festival at North Seattle Community College, where Billie was invited to have a table promoting her fair trade coffee shop. She gave coffee samples and I set up a Mini Etching press for printing a two-color print from an etched copper plate.

People were encouraged to put their name on the print and—later on when the ink was dry—come to the Blue Saucer to claim their personalized, free print. The hope, of course, was that the claimant would buy something.

The card layout and design resembling a commercial Collectible Trading Card but with the provenance of the edition of prints. For preparing for etching the plate, Nellie Sunderland, Billie's sister, made a stipple drawing of the Cerulean

Warbler, the bird which was chosen because it is a native of the same region in Central America where the Blue Saucer's fair trade coffee grows.

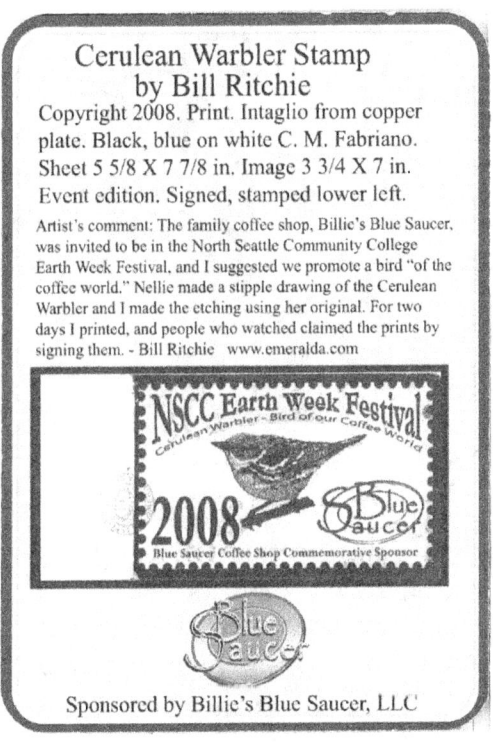

Figure 6: Cerulean Warbler artiststamp, an Earth Day 2008 commemorative. This illustration is approximately the actual size, as artists' collectible trading cards usually measure 2 ½ inches wide and 3 ½ inches high.

Artists Collectible Trading Cards

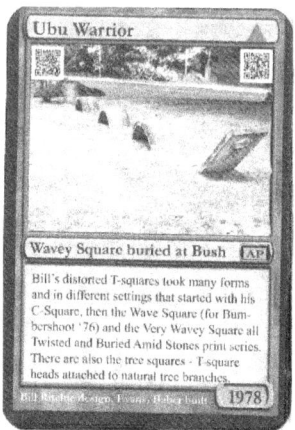 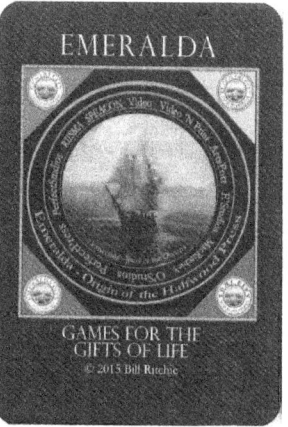

Figure 7: Wavey Square Buried at Bush, one sample of the four cards, the layout and design of which resemble commercial trading cards for games.

4 Wavey Square Buried at Bush School

An experiment for the *ArtistRIPStock*, where four cards represent an artist's asset up for sale as a stock certificate. The sculpture, *Wavey Square Buried*, was made in 1978 by summer session students at the Helen Bush School in Seattle.

Dennis Evans and Bill Baber were the teachers. They asked me to contribute a design from my *Wave Square Series* so that their students could have an experience making a cast concrete project involving shop equipment and form-building. By the year 2000, the original sculpture, which is made in 5 parts, had been moved to an open space alongside the street and it is visible both from this street and, on computers, by satellite.

The physical Artists Collectible Trading Cards has four images of the sculpture, some taken with me in them. QR codes might take the user to Google Maps and locate the sculpture on screen in street and satellite views.

In this deck I included colored triangles to represent the colors of the four Women Who Fell to Earth, often referenced in my stories and in the Emeralda Legend. Each of the four cards in this deck have the initials AP, which stands for ArtsPort, one of the islands of domains of expertise in the imaginary Emeralda region.

The words, *Ubu Warrior*, appear in the top bar, referring to Dennis Evans, who used the pseudonym, *Ubu*, for many years in performances, installations and visual artworks. Warrior is adopted from *Magic: The Gathering*, which always served as a metaphor for my game design quest.

The text, in parts that span four cards, tells the story of the Evans/Baber project and the idea behind the *Very Wavy Square*. In one corner the date—1978—is given as the year this sculpture was made.

The backs of four of the seven remaining cards from this set are different from the one shown in figure 7. They are from the first iteration of the card design. The illustration shown above is on three cards and it is the design used on the Emeralda game box—the same as was used in Number 9, following, and shown in Figure 20, and as a computer screen wallpaper—Figure 21.

The ship in the center is the Emeralda, subject of my stories about a fated ship which brought to me the design of the Halfwood press line. Around the ship image is a circle of the ten islands' names, the four cities of Emeralda Region, and the title.

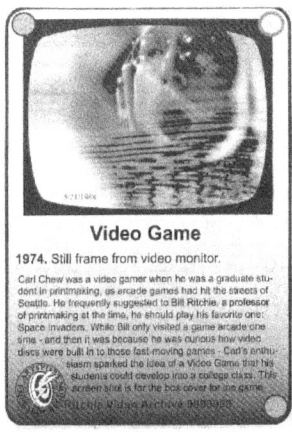
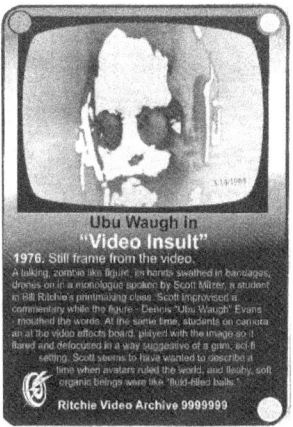

Figure 8: Two selected sample cards for Video Dig Reloaded, a video art installation in an art museum, a Trading Card Game, and an interactive APP..

5 Video Dig Reloaded

At a party in 2012 I was re-introduced the then-new director of a local art museum. We actually had met 40 years before in connection with a video art show she directed in Vancouver, BC. We reminisced about the good old days when video art was new and we were doing innovative things with video at Seattle's UW and in British Columbia.

"We should bring back the spirit of those times," she said. I took the comment as a hint, and it fired me up to, once again, attempt restoration of the archive of videos I have from the 1970s. The theme, *Video Dig Reloaded*, refers to an art event

Artists Collectible Trading Cards

and installation by C. T. Chew of which we have the original black-and-white video documentation.

In a letter to the museum director I suggested that a video installation would be more interesting if it was accompanied with an interactive game. The video installations I have seen are boring—like watching someone's home movies. Then I wrote a book about it.

It was my intent to bring about a mini-course on the history of electronic arts in the northwest, using this show to set the tone of keeping the video art in a relationship to its successor—video games.

I steamed along for months, making these cards, refreshing my database and producing a self-published paperback book to explain the concept in depth. I sent her a copy. Strangely, there was no response—no interest shown at all.

In time, she replaced the then-current curator of contemporary art with a new man. At my first opportunity I visited him and told the *Video Dig Reloaded* story how I still hoped to get a video show going at this museum; and I gave him a book, too—my last copy.

In over three years, I never heard any more about it. Apparently, the chat we had at that party in 2012 was just "party talk." The idea is still alive, for me, and the trading card deck is still one of the best card decks I made.

I made sample cards for my pitch to the art museum director so that a trading card game could be combined with an installed exhibition. It would be sold in the museum shop, of course. An online interactive game or APP could accompanying it, and be another way to get money for the project.

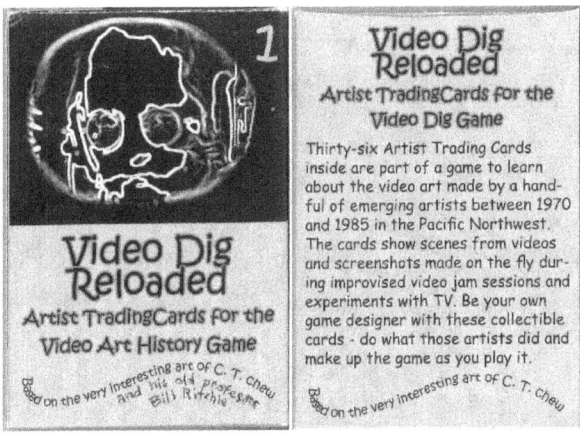

Figure 9: Front and back sides of the box for the deck of cards for *Video Dig Reloaded*.

The cards

In the first deck there were 64 cards—eight sets of 8 duplicates; however some are missing. Eight cards were originally printed, having only one side, in color, on glossy card stock. The reader may wonder, *Why are there eight cards and not, say, seven, or fifteen?* The answer is that my technique for making cards uses common printing services,

Artists Collectible Trading Cards

such as FedEx Kinkos. I don't keep a color printer, which would be too expensive to feed and maintain.

Color laser printing is ideal as the machines print formats in 8 ½ X 11 and 11 X 17 inch glossy card stock. One sheet can hold four to eight cards—depending on whether the cards are two-sided or one-sided. The larger sheet can print 8 to 16 cards!

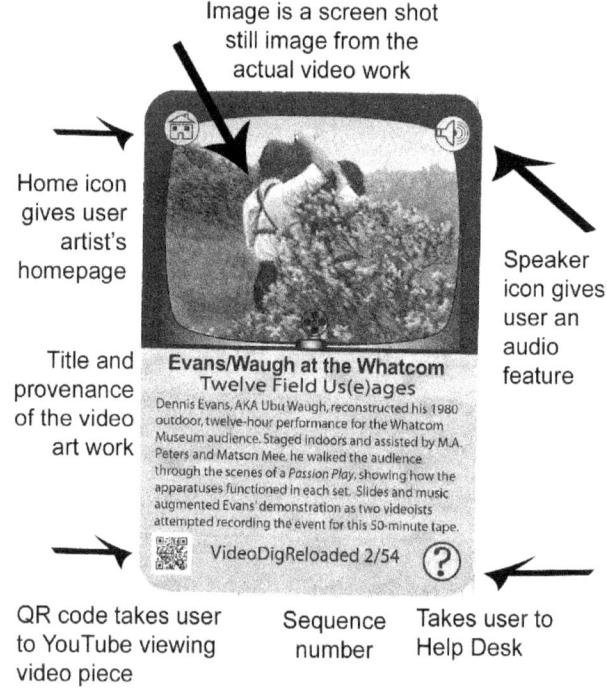

Figure 10: Anatomy of the Video Dig Reloaded card

The back story would be adapted from my students' and my roles in pioneering video art in the Northwest, given a fictional scope to provide an adventure aspect of our exploration and experiments with TV as art.

The video art pieces I selected From my archive for my plan numbered 48, therefore the deck for the Trading Card Game would have at least 48 cards, which I figured would extend to 54 or more, or four times that number depending what the game mechanic required, and extensions that might come along later when the game matured.

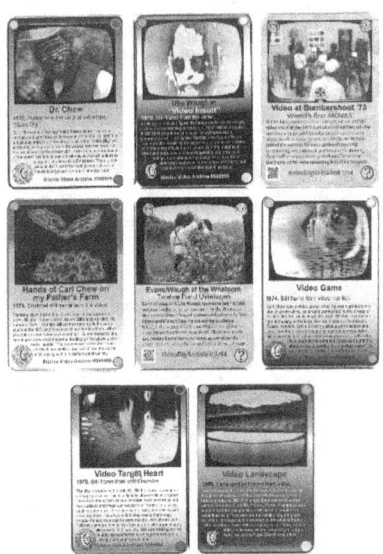

Figure 11: Eight of 54 cards for Video Dig created as samples to show how a Trading Card Game to accompany a museum video art installation.

Artists Collectible Trading Cards

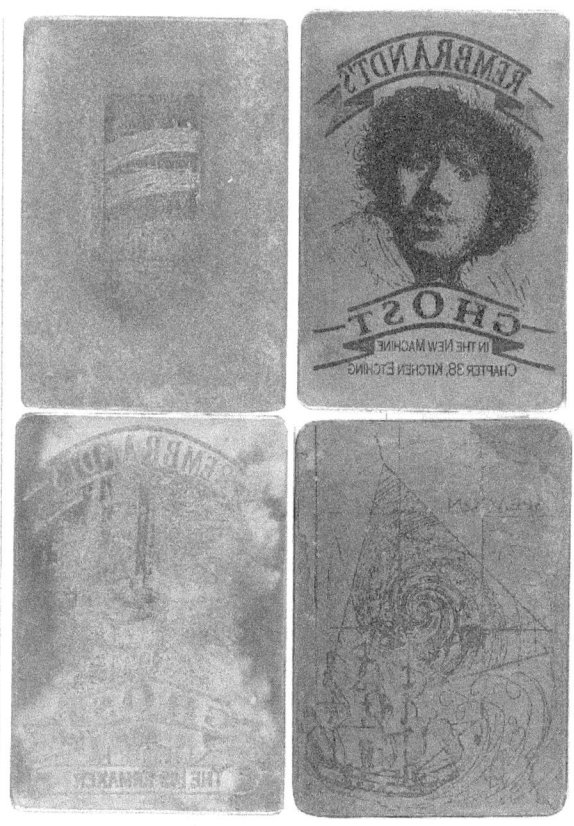

Figure 12: Copper Plates selected from the etchings to print Artists Collectible Trading Cards.

6 Copper Plates

These copperplate etchings are for printing Artist Collectible Trading Cards on an etching press. It is conceivable, however, that the plates are collectible as they are—with or without the prints that have come from them.

Three series are represented in the image above. Clockwise beginning with the top left plate, there are three from the Artist's Stamps. I etched designs I chose from my collections of my artworks as artistamps (spanning 50-years) in 22-gauge copper plate cut to the same size as CTC.

The year was 2008, and I made this in anticipation of a workshop I was invited to present in Kansas at Baker University. Professor Walt Bailey set up a series of workshops, and for the one to be given to students at the upper class level I made these plates and I left all but three with the students who succeeded in printing them.

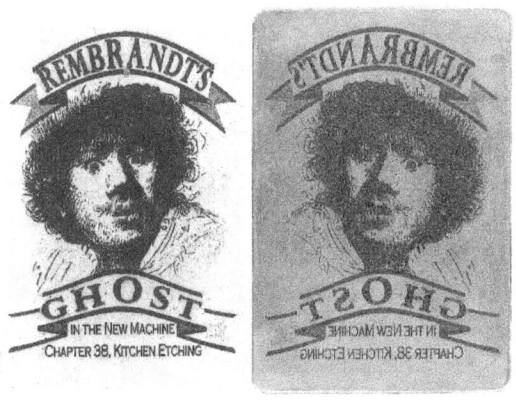

Figure 13: Four of the existing plates are for the game to be based on the novel, Rembrandt's Ghost in the New

Artists Collectible Trading Cards

Machine. This one is for Chapter 38, *Kitchen Etching*, shown here with a proof from the copper plate.

The second selection shown is from the Rembrandt's Ghost series. This example, which is one of four extant plates, shows the image from the often-reproduced, *Self Portrait in a Cap* of Rembrandt. Other cards in this series use images I made for each chapter of my novel, *Rembrandt's Ghost in the New Machine*. If I were to continue this series I would make fifty-four printing plates.

The third plate in the four-plate image is also from the *Rembrandt's Ghost* series. It's for Chapter one and depicting a paper maker at work. I wrote the novel with the intention to use it for the back story of a game based on Rembrandt's self-portraits (his *selfies*, as one person quipped).

The lower right plate in Figure 12 is from a series I made to go with my suite of games, *Emeralda: Games for the Gifts of Life*. This series is from 2005—a time when I was experimenting with etching plates fused with laser toner as an etching ground with mixed results; but despite the flaws in the process—which left strange marks and splotchy shapes—I liked their imperfections because they looked like they had been corroded over a long time—like images of artifacts found in undersea shipwrecks.

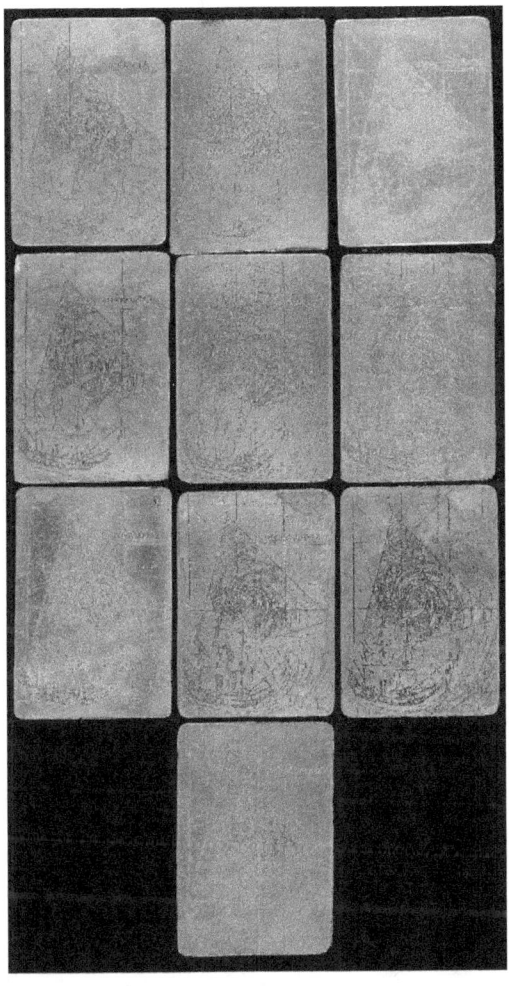

Figure 14: Ten etched copper plates from 2005 with one card for each island of domain-of-expertise in Emeralda.

Artists Collectible Trading Cards

The legend of the mystery frigate, the *Emeralda*, was serving my development of a Halfwood Press marketing theme. Added to this was the triangle, reminiscent of the Bermuda Triangle mythology except that I placed in my imaginary place, Emeralda Region.

Ten islands in the great, bottomless lake of Emeralda Region make up my imaginary place, and so there are ten plates, each one bearing the name of the island it represents. Most of the etched copper plates have only a front side image but a few have dates engraved on the back.

Using various colors, in addition to black ink, I printed all ten plates in 2005-2006 and, much later, I assembled them into an artist's book. I made only one, and Professor Mann, at Baker University, bought it from the show which Professor Bailey arranged for me. Many of the plates still have the ink dried into them; I was so busy making presses and boxes for them that making plates and printing them became a pleasant and distracting pastime—almost therapeutic.

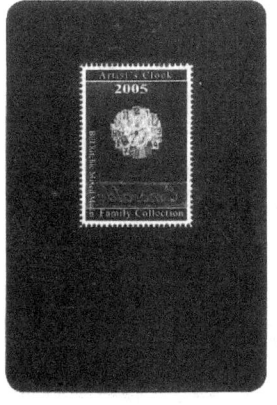 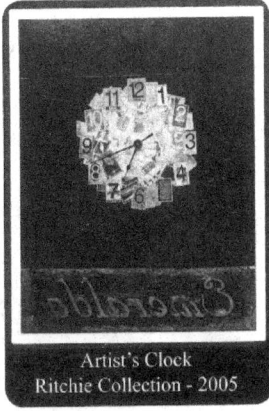

Figure 15: Artist's Clock, a 2006 work made for a fund-raising event celebrating the career of a Seattle art maven, Anne Focke. Cards are in three versions.

7 Artist's Clock

The Artist's Clock project began when I was invited to donate a work with a clock in it for an event celebrating Anne Focke's long, rich career in Seattle. I made two clocks and both of them were sold at the auction—the benefits going to a community service, I believe.

I liked those two clocks, so I made one more for myself. Its face is a collage of my artist's stamps from 1960-2000, mounted on the surface of a black canvas-covered box painted black.

Later I added a woodcut that I had made for a print with the word *Emeralda* carved in. Of course,

Artists Collectible Trading Cards

the word *Emeralda* is backward since it's a direct print. To keep the dust off I got an acrylic box for it.

I made my Artist Collectible Trading Cards for Artist's Clock are in three variations. Two are tent folders with its story on one side, and the third is in the design I planned to use for gallery labels.

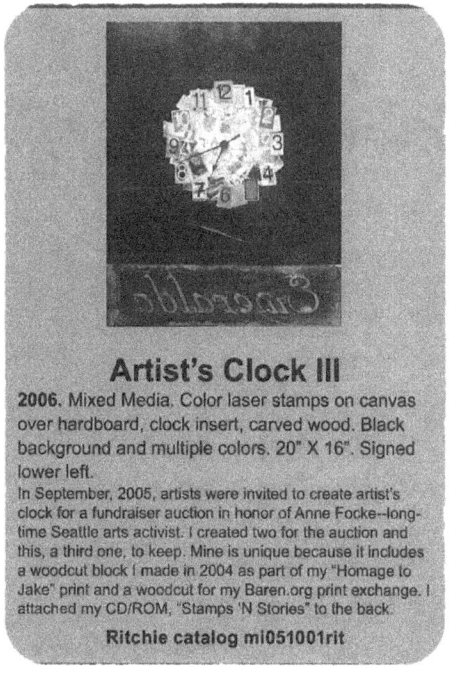

Figure 16: The card version intended to be label for the clock displayed in the Ritchie Family Gallery.

On the back of the box I taped on an envelope and inserted in it my 2004 CD/ROM project,

Stamps 'N Stories, which would provide the owner of this Artist's Clock with the entire collection of artistamps up to 2003 and would serve to explain the plan I had for an interactive game based on artistamps.

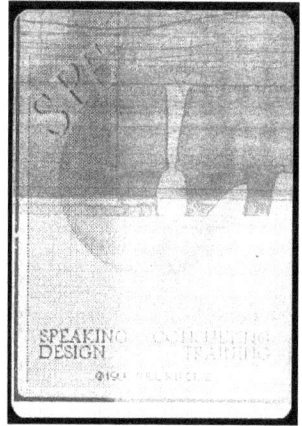 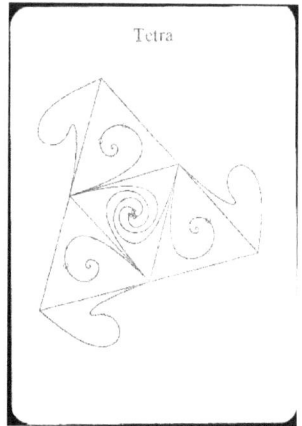

Figure 17: SPEACON Deck, sample image of art side, left, and, right, the back or common side of all the cards. The name, "Tetra," on this example, is one of the four suits on the cards, from the Emeralda mythology.

8 SPEACON Deck

Ten island domains-of-expertise figure on the Great Lake of Emeralda Region, and this deck is played on SPEACON, Domain-of-Expertise (DoE) in public Speaking, Consulting, Design and Training.

The front side of card is a cut-up print I made for the Seattle Sheraton Hotel project in the 1980s, one of two lithographs commissioned by the hotel. By calculation I got fifty-four cards by cutting the print to the size that fit my printer, and then cutting up the sections to get nine cards each sheet to the size of the standard Artist Trading Card.

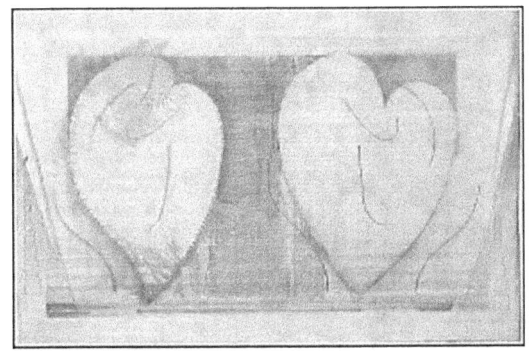

Figure 18: The print which was cut up into trading cards after the SPEACON logo was printed on side and the Tetrahedron template was printed on the back, white side. The print is a six-color offset lithograph printed as part the then-new Seattle Sheraton Hotel project.

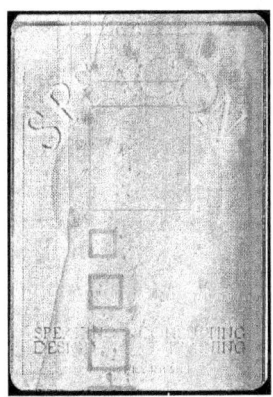

Figure 19: Another of the SPEACON domain-of-expertise in Speaking, Consulting, Design and Training cards—the color of the right-side, an edge indicating where it would be in the make-up of the entire print.

Artists Collectible Trading Cards

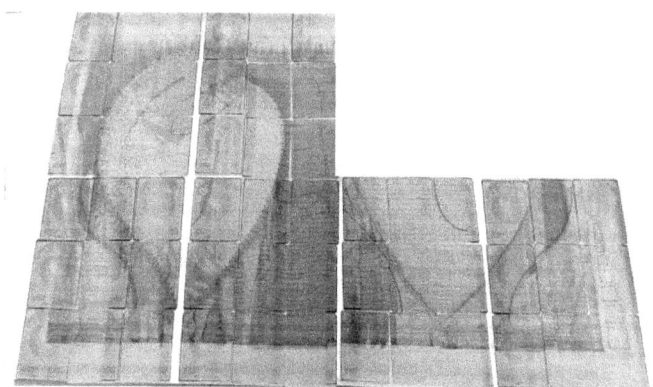

Figure 20: The original print is about 22 X 30 inches and yielded six sheets of 8 ½ X 11 to produce fifty-four trading cards for the deck.

The printing of the SPEACON logo, in black, is faint; and it is in a gradient—fading out so, on some cards, it fades out. This is accidental. In the days when making these cards, I didn't have much money. Toner cartridges were around $75 at the time and I couldn't replace my laser toner cartridges when they ran low—often using the "shake-it-up" method to yield as much toner as possible.

In one variation, there are six decks of nine cards each that, when fitted together, reconstruct the image of the 8 ½ X 11-inch original section of the cut-up print. It's like putting together a puzzle except they do not interlock, jigsaw-style.

Suits

As with another deck made from cutting up my print (Number 1 in this book, the *Poster Deck*) one side of the cards relates to the Emeralda mythology. The four *Women-who-fell-to-Earth*—Aurel, Media, Techne and Tetra are given thirteen cards each and there are two Omnium Gatherum cards.

These four suits, one for each of the women from the Emeralda Legend, approximate the suits of typical Poker decks, i.e, heart, spade, diamond and club. The Omnium Gatherum cards may be thought of as Jokers; but usually I think of them as standing for the two brothers in the sextuplet of aliens.

Artists Collectible Trading Cards

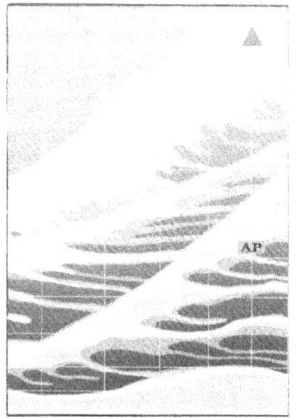 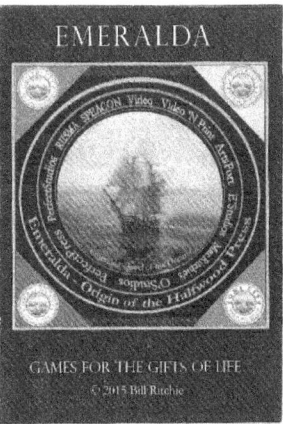

Figure 21: Emeralda deck one side based on the map of the part of Lake Powell, Arizona, where a scene was filmed for the first *Planet of the Apes movie*. The other based on the box for *Emeralda Suite*.

9 Emeralda cards

Sixteen of these cards fit together to make a small version (10 X 14 inches) *Cyanotype 1980* poster image which, in turn, is based on my prints from the series, *Spaceship Crash* (inspired by a scene from the original, first movie, *Planet of the Apes*). This series included cyanotype process prints, and from one I selected the image for a six-color offset poster.

In Figure 20 above, the card shown at the left is cut from the lower right corner of the poster in Figure 21, below—above the title bar.

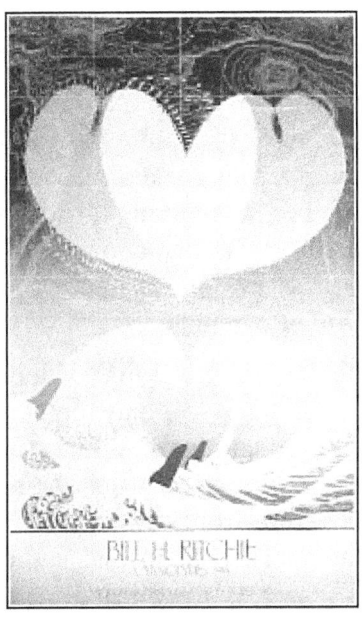

Figure 22: The original, 6-color offset poster is large by poster standards, about 26 X 42 inches. In this deck, only the map image area comes into play, and when assembled, the poster is about 1/3 the full size.

On the sixteen cards in this deck I put tiny colored triangles to represent the four *Women-who-fell-to-Earth*. These "muses" come from my *Emeralda* mythology—the imaginary place I architected in the '90s (this resource is referred to in Numbers 1 and 8, above). It was this point in my efforts to invent an Artists Collectible Trading Card game I was trying to figure out how to use a scoring system so as to make the cards playable.

In addition to the triangles I put the letters AP, which is the acronym for ArtsPort, one of the ten Islands-of-domains-of-Expertise. Again, in numbers 1 and 8, above, the islands are part of the mythical Emeralda Region, and ArtsPort is the Domain-of-expertise-in-Cyber-navigation. The idea came originally meant knowledge about getting around in disk operating systems and the ports or connections in the hardware of computers.

The back, or common, side of the deck is the design for the Emeralda game box. It's also the wallpaper for my computer screens, put there to stimulate my thinking about what the real, physical box—if there ever is one—would contain. I made such a box, about 12 X 12 inches, and deep enough to contain cards, board and game pieces.

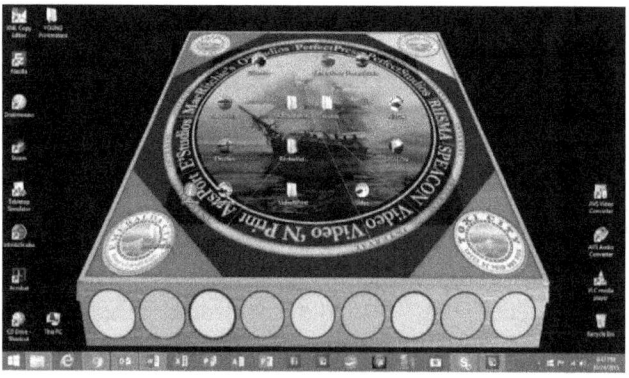

Figure 23: The Emeralda game box and computer screen wallpaper that served for the common backs of this deck.

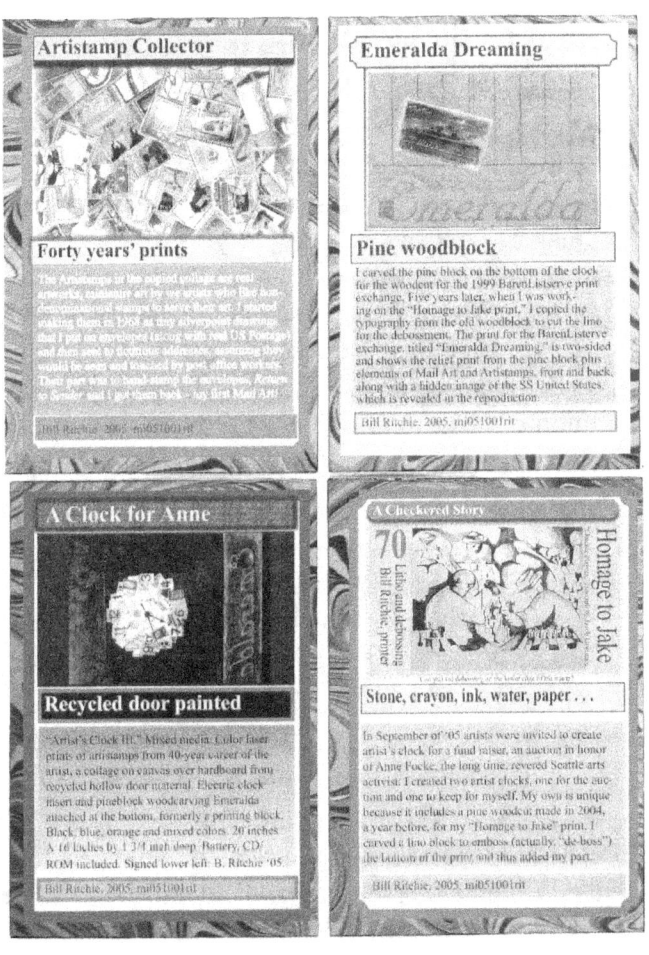

Figure 24: Emeralda Dreaming, four cards make up the deck for this experiment for ArtistsRIPStock, a system for converting artists' assets into shares in a B-Corp to monetize artists' projects for community development.

10 Emeralda Dreaming

Emeralda Dreaming is the title of this deck based on a print I made in 2005 for my participation in a Baren.org print exchange. These kinds of exchanges had been going on for years among printmakers—aided greatly by the Web. I participated in two or three in this online organization for printmakers who specialize in relief printing in the Japanese manner using the antique printing tool, the *baren*. The print is exchange is a common practice in print clubs all over the world.

I chose this artwork for a deck in an experiment for the *ArtistRIPStock*, where four cards represent an artist's asset which is up for sale as a stock certificate in a Social Purpose Corporation, or B-Corp (Benefit Corporation). *ArtistsRIPStock* focuses on this mixed media print titled, *Emeralda Dreaming*.

There are four cards in an *ArtistsRIPStock* deck. On one side, the relevant data about the item—known in the art collecting world as the artwork's *Provenance*—is nested in up to sixteen fields. Fifteen are reserved for the data side, and the sixteenth is for the art side—the other side which is actually a likeness of the artwork divided into four quadrants. In a deck, a total of 64 field are possible.

When the four cards are aligned with the likeness' quadrants, the viewer has a 5 X 7 inch reproduction of the item, for which the share is bought and owned by the collector—or collectors. It is possible for several people to divide ownership of a share of *ArtistsRIPStock*.

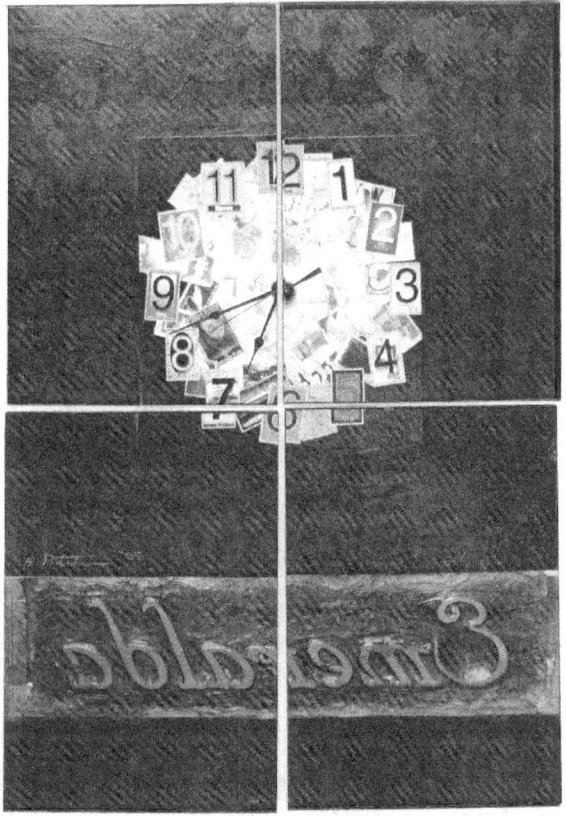

Figure 25: The verso of the data sides of the stock, this one being fitted together so that a small reproduction is given to the owner—or owners.

Artists Collectible Trading Cards

Connected cards

Goethe observed, Connect, always connect. I followed this dictum many years, thinking how everything is connected, and this deck is an example. The Artist's Clock is referenced in another, older deck (Number 7, above).

In all my artwork in my 50-year career up to the present there are connections, like a great web or fabric, with one event or experience leading to another, and sometimes looping back recursively.

One of the card games I bought used this connectivity by physically placing cards' edges next to each other if they showed a certain characteristic, such as a symbol, a color, or number. Possibly this notion, *connect, always connect*, is inherent in game play. In my later years, I restated Goethe with, *Interfere, always interfere*.

This got me into a lot of trouble, I should mention. Yet, it came in handy when I was trying understand the realities guiding human kind and in science. So, it may be true, too, in designing cards for my life game, *Emeralda*.

ArtistsRIPStock-the name

I arrived at the name (as it is now, at the time of this writing) *ArtistsRIPStock* at about the same time my wife and I were updating our wills. For a long time I have been concerned about dying without having arranged for the disposal of our art collection. Since our collection spans many media and centers mostly on me as an artist and teacher, I fear that our entire collection may be destined to go to the landfill.

People are shocked and somewhat amazed by this idea, but because I never strived for fame as an artist, playing the art game as it were, I sometimes think it is likely the landfill is where it will go. We are, after all, a wasteful nation, and cultural arts are no exception—particularly if ill-fit for popular socio-economic frameworks.

Many artists must face this likelihood, and if it were not for, at the same time as writing my will: I worked on starting the *Northwest Print Center and Incubators*. Funding this ambitious project will be difficult, I think—particularly since my idea is, "a vast notion with a half-vast plan."

To people who have given this some thought, the way to use the art collection is the proven art auction. However, I've seen too many art auctions; and others, also, have seen too many art auctions and they no longer find them appealing.

In fact, the people who have gone to art auctions over the past two generations have bought all the art they can store or display. Many are trying to get rid of their accumulated art; they have donated their art to non-profits, museums, schools and clubs or offered it to their children and friends.

Storage is the problem many art collectors face, not to mention maintenance and valuation. New art

Artists Collectible Trading Cards

buyers—such as the thousands of workers moving to Seattle and furnishing their apartments—are pressed for time or they don't want expensive work that encumbers their next move.

The idea of a miniature storage system for works of art, and also which can be digitally access appeals to me. Turning art into stock is a solution; I wrote a book about it a couple years ago, in fact. However, as I face the fact of my death, I want to find peace of mind. Writing a will, for an artist who is not famous and collectible, invites tears, knowing a life's work will be destroyed and forgotten.

In my years of travel and teaching, I met a few old artists—in their 70s, 80s, and 90s—who made the same lament. They had a small degree of international fame, but they didn't want to see their accomplishments die and be forgotten. After so much work and sacrifice, it would be sad, they said.

RIP means *Rest in Peace*, so, in humor, I made up the name *ArtistsRIPStock*. It happens, too, "rip stock" is a type of fabric that resists tearing. It was developed in World War II for parachutes; now it's used for yacht sails, kites, hot-air balloons, flags, camping tents and much more.

I would "rest in peace" if I invent a way to dispose of our entire collection and finance the *Northwest Print Center and Incubators*.

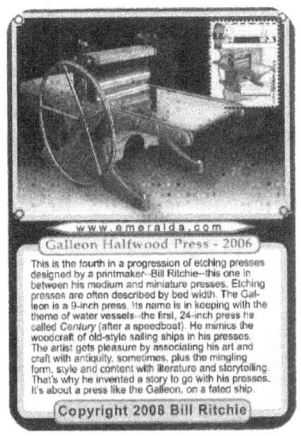 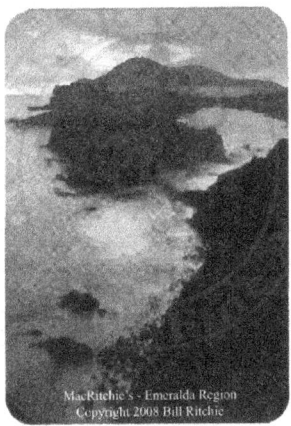

Figure 26: Galleon Halfwood Press was one of the decks I made for the Halfwood Press line—this one for the 9-inch model, the Galleon. The back side uses the ArtsPort image, with a faint imprint of the ArtsPort logo.

11 Galleon Halfwood Press

The face of the card mimics cards for *Magic: The Gathering* with its placement of image, text and small title bars. The text carries the story of the press – its history, for example, being the fourth of the Halfwood presses I made between 2004 and 2008. The text says:

Artists Collectible Trading Cards

> "This is the fourth in a progression of etching presses designed by a printmaker – Bill Ritchie – this one in between his medium and miniature presses. Etching presses are often described by bed width. The Galleon is a 9-inch press. Its name is in keeping with the theme of water vessels – the first 24-inch press he called Century (after a speedboat). He mimics the woodcraft of old-style sailing ships in his presses. The artist gets pleasure by associating his art and craft with antiquity, sometimes, plus the mingling form, style and content with literature and storytelling. That's why he invented a story to go with his presses. It's about a press like the Galleon, on a fated ship."

There are five models of the Halfwood line of printmaking presses I designed, and when I was coming up with ways to promote a printmaking teaching method using games, I designed cards for the presses. This one is for the Galleon Halfwood Press, which at the time was the biggest one with a 9-inch wide press. Small, by industrial standards, but a perfect size for small studios.

There are twenty-seven cards in this deck, more or less identical. Decks of playing cards often number 54, counting two Jokers; this deck might be "half" of a full deck. The upper right corner of the image area has what I intended to be a miniature artistamp, a commemorative artistamp for the Galleon. It so happened that the file was corrupted, and when I sent it to the printer, the image of the stamp was garbled and the cards differ from one another. I conserved them, regardless.

The verso, common, side of the cards shows a rocky island a little off shore. This photo caught my eye as a potential illustration for my meta-game, *Emeralda: Games for the gifts of life*. The print on the bottom edge says this island is *MacRitchie's*, one of ten Islands-of-Domains-of-Expertise I give to the imaginary place where Emeralda's back story takes place. In other cards, above, cards were made for SPEACON and ArtsPort – others among the ten islands on the *Great Lake of Emeralda Region.* Careful examination of the image of the island reveals the logo for MacRitchie's faintly overprinted on the island picture.

Halfwood presses are made in Emeralda Region, an imaginary world for the back story in Emeralda Mythology. This is an interesting strategic plan in the making of Halfwood Presses as this is destined to become a profitable enterprise. The mythical world becomes the Bible for the marketing of the presses. Add to this the potential of a Collectible Trading Card game and it gains more interest.

Artists Collectible Trading Cards

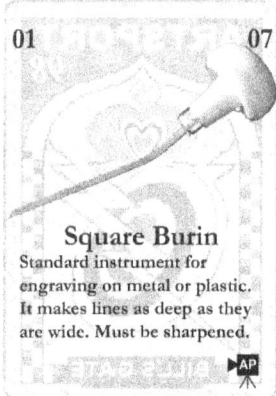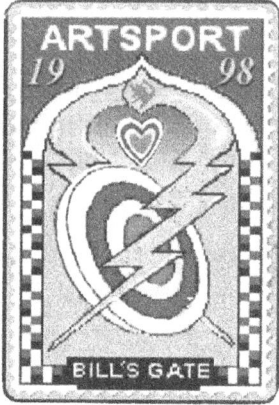

Figure 27: Printmaker Genius card, the data side and the side common to all the cards.

12 Printmaker Genius Sample

It was 2011 when I made this set of cards. My scanner and software were outdated, so the image is pixelated. They are part of work on the rules for *Escape Emeralda*, inspired by a Hidden Object Game (HOG) titled *Escape the Emerald Star*. The purpose of *Escape Emeralda* was to define or identify 100 items in the printmaking workshop and either win your freedom or locate the missing professor to whose tutelage you had been assigned as an apprentice.

This deck focused on the engraver's tool, the square burin, as an example of one of one-hundred items that make up a complete printmaker's workshop. This was a trial run of the trading cards, and on the back is this explanation:

> This is an example of an Artist Trading Card for the game, *Escape Emeralda*. The number on the upper left shows it is from the first Island Domain-of-Expertise known as ArtsPort: The DOE in cyberspace navigation. The number on the upper right indicates the object number, the 7th object of the total ten objects. The first ten objects are in the Studio of the Missing Professor's residence on ArtsPort. The Image is of the object – a burin. The text below the object defines it. Below the text, on the lower right, is a "bug" that indicates there is a video for this object, ranging in length from five to sixty seconds' duration. The faded background image is reverse of the ArtsPort Deck of forty cards of images (plus 14 other types of cards for ArtsPort.) in110907. Note: this sample is filed in the Interval directory for 2011.

Eight cards make up this deck. Four are like the one illustrated above, two have the ArtsPort banner with the text on the verso, and two have the burin image on one side and the text on the verso.

Artists Collectible Trading Cards

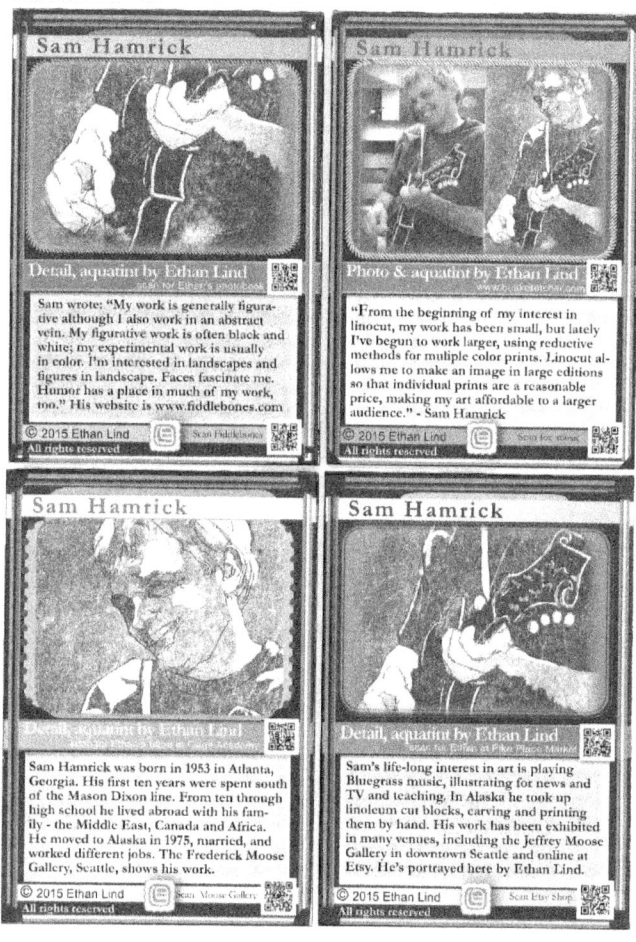

Figure 28: Sam Hamrick, a deck of four cards, an experiment to showcase artists who practice printmaking and performing arts using information collected on the artist's website.

13 Sam Hamrick

Sam is an artist and musician in Seattle, known for his linoleum cuts that usually feature skeletons in comical positions and antics. He calls his work, *fiddle-bones*. He plays mandolin with bluegrass bands around the region and he also teaches printmaking.

This card is an experiment to learn how to get information a designer needs to make a trading card using only the artist's website for data.

Four cards comprise the deck. One side shows an etched portrait of Sam by his friend, another blue grass musician (a banjo player), named Ethan Lind. Ethan, a printmaker, painter, and teacher, is also known as the Busker Etcher.

Details about the print and Sam himself make up one side of each of the four cards. It is the data side and images include Ethan's original snapshot. Ethan often works from snapshots of musicians performing, and he composed his etching of Sam from this snapshot.

The other side of the print is the actual size print (about 5 x 7 inches) cut into in four quadrants so that the cards can be assembled to make up the whole image.

Artists Collectible Trading Cards

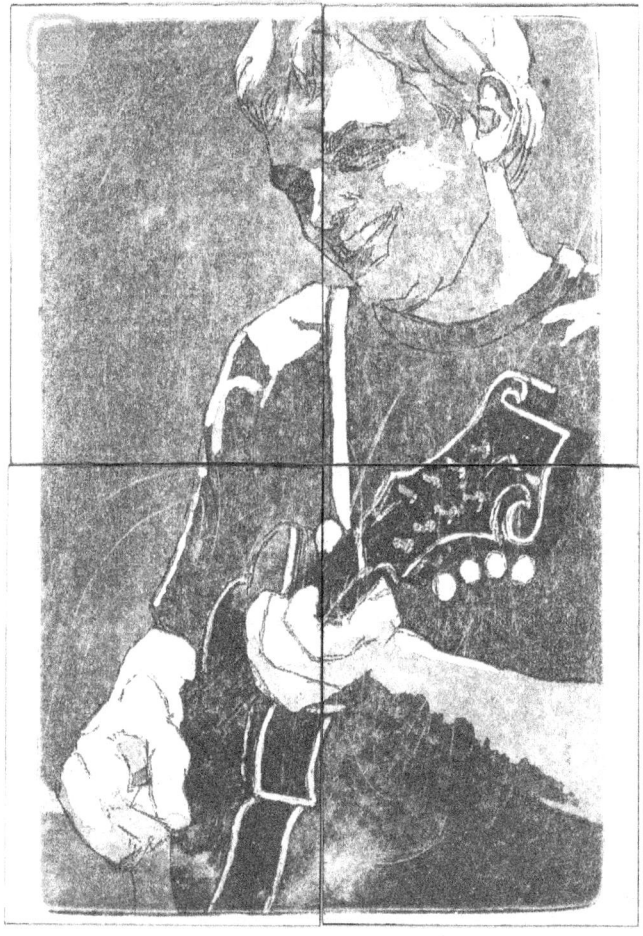

Figure 29: Verso, or art side, of the Sam Hamrick deck of four cards. The cards assembled in this way provide a reasonable facsimile the actual size of the original.

Sam Hamrick was born in 1953 in Atlanta, Georgia. His first ten years were spent south of the Mason Dixon line. From ten through high school he lived abroad with his family - the Middle East, Canada and Africa. He moved to Alaska in 1975, married, and worked different jobs. The Frederick Moose Gallery, Seattle, shows his work.

Sam's life-long interest in art is playing Bluegrass music, illustrating for news and TV and teaching. In Alaska he took up linoleum cut blocks, carving and printing them by hand. His work has been exhibited in many venues, including the Jeffrey Moose Gallery in downtown Seattle and online at Etsy. He's portrayed here by Ethan Lind.

Text boxes give information from Sam's website.

"From the beginning of my interest in linocut, my work has been small, but lately I've begun to work larger, using reductive methods for multiple color prints. Linocut allows me to make an image in large editions so that individual prints are a reasonable price, making my art affordable to a larger audience." - Sam Hamrick

Sam wrote: "My work is generally figurative although I also work in an abstract vein. My figurative work is often black and white; my experimental work is usually in color. I'm interested in landscapes and figures in landscape. Faces fascinate me. Humor has a place in much of my work, too." His website is www.fiddlebones.com

Artists Collectible Trading Cards

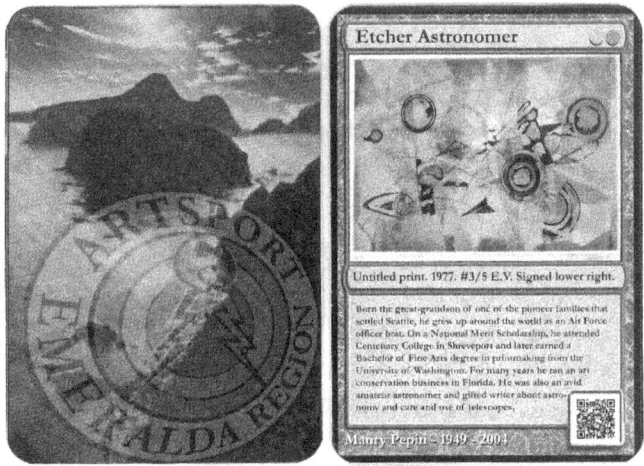

Figure 30: Pepin Etcher/Astronomer card, one of four comprising the deck, back or common side and data side. This is state 1 of the cards, as more information has since come available.

14 Pepin-Etcher/astronomer

Maury Pepin was a student in my etching classes at the University of Washington, and he died young. It was in the days when I kept a print from each of a few exceptional students to show newcomers. I returned most of them before I left the UW, but I had no contact information Maury until the Web search came. Too late, for I learned he had died of an infection.

I made a deck of four cards. One side is identical across all four. The back, or common side, is different but similar to the one shown, using the

ArtsPort portal image and the logo. I used these in some above, Numbers 11 and 12, too.

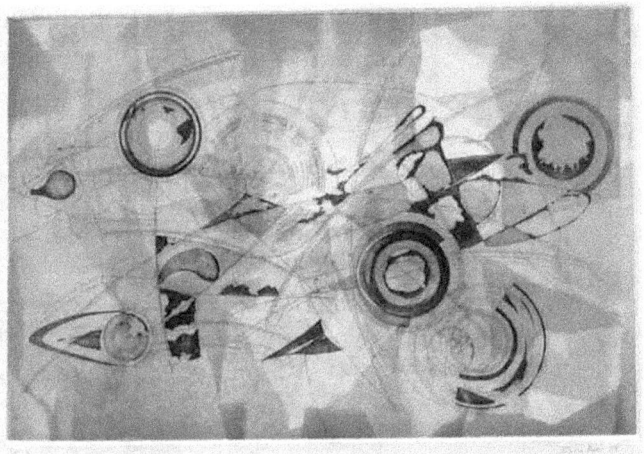

Figure 31: The original print by Maury Pepin which provides the image for the cards and, reassembled, yields a small, 4-part production of the print.

The text box says:

> Born the great grandson of one of the pioneer families that settled Seattle, he grew up around the world as an Air Force office brat. On a National Merit Scholarship, he attended Centenary College in Shreveport and later earned a Bachelor of Fine Arts degree in printmaking from the University of Washington. For many years he ran an art conservation business in Florida. He was also an avid amateur astronomer and gifted writer about astronomy and care and use of telescopes.

I continued to add to the design of the card, having found an image of his grave marker, and this would, if I pursue it, lead to more variations on the card.

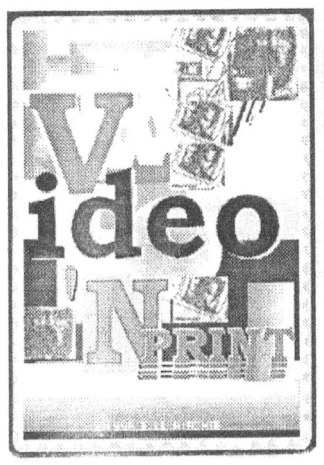 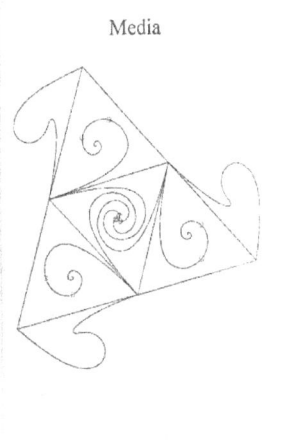

Media

Figure 32: Video 'N Print deck, like two examples given in 1 and 8, above, is from the first experiments to make a game based on the mythical Emeralda Region. This black-and-white test deck has the tetrahedron pattern on the suit-side; the one shown here is the *Media* series.

15 Video 'N Print

Ten island domains-of-expertise dot the *Great Lake of Emeralda Region*. The Video'N Print deck is played on *Video 'N Print*, Domain-of-Expertise in, "Video production extended to printmaking or printer-friendly interface systems." Roughly translated, this means knowing how to make stop-action or screen shots and resolve them to print media, such as etching, woodcut, screen print and lithography.

Artists Collectible Trading Cards

When you visit this island, you find the culture exists entirely around converting video to hard copy, usually with a lot of handcraft involved.

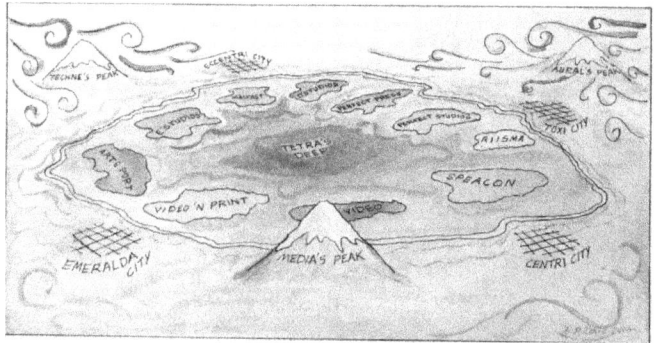

Figure 33: Watercolor sketch of the Great Lake of Emeralda region, with its four mountains (three are visible on land, one is inverted underwater), ten islands, and four city-state capitols.

Fifty-four cards make the deck and, like the other, the laser printer was running out of toner. The common or "back" of the card is fading out on many cards. The four suits are allocated to thirteen cards each for the four *Women who Fell to Earth* in the *Emeralda Legend*.

Two cards remain for the two brothers—the Good and the Evil—who complete the alien sextuplet. Think of these two un-labeled cards as the Jokers of a traditional playing card deck.

Also on this side is the paper cut-and-fold tetrahedron pattern—tetrahedrons being the building blocks of the alien's spacecraft.

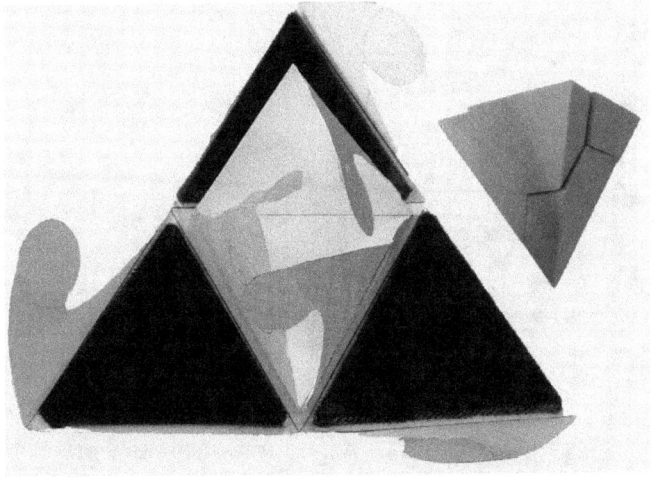

Figure 34: The pattern on the cards is the tetrahedron paper cut-and-fold design. Shown in this figure the tetrahedron is open, showing another, open nested tetrahedron inside. At the right is a plastic puzzle toy that forms a solid tetrahedron. This paper tetrahedron is lined with green velvet.

The paper stock of this issue is heavy, printed one side on recycled file folders and the other side printed on regular copy paper and pasted on the tag stock. To achieve this weight paper, it would be too heavy to have been fed through the printer. Only hand-printing would result in this weight.

Artists Collectible Trading Cards

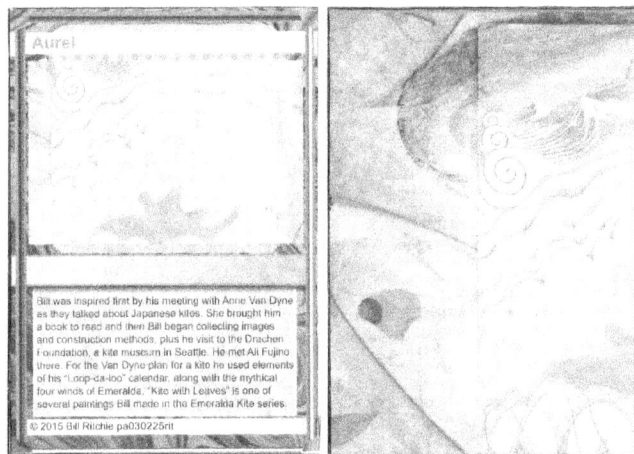

Figure 35: Kite with Leaves is based on a painting I made in 2003 in acrylic. The design is the trading card style, left, and the backs of the cards each have a quadrant of the painting which, fitted together, make a 5 X 7 inch reproduction.

16 Kite with Leaves

Kite with Leaves is a deck of four cards based on my 2003 painting of the same title. The trading card layout has a text block, each one containing the details of the artwork, artist's statement, provenance, and ephemeral text.

The upper left of each card is allocated to one of the four *Women who Fell to Earth* from the *Emeralda Legend*, and at the bottom is listed the Ritchie Art Catalog number—pa030225rit—which indicates that the painting was completed on February 25, 2003.

You can detect some portion of the full image (at the right) on the face of the one example of the data side of the card (at the left) being near the center part of the artwork.

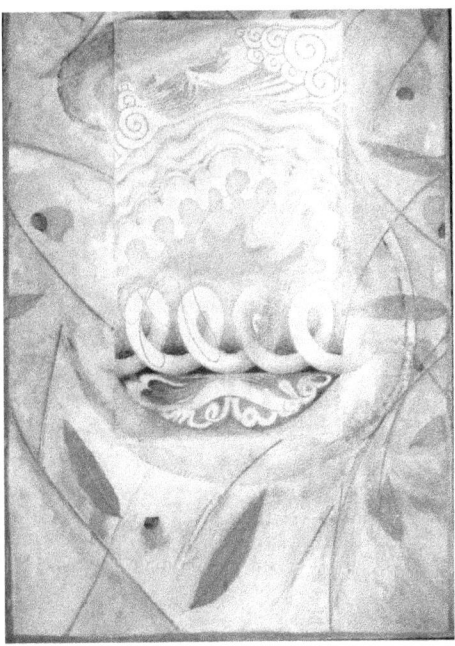

Figure 36: "Kite with Leaves," the original painting on which the deck of four cards is made. When the four cards in the deck are arranged, you have a 5 X 7 inch reproduction.

Artists Collectible Trading Cards

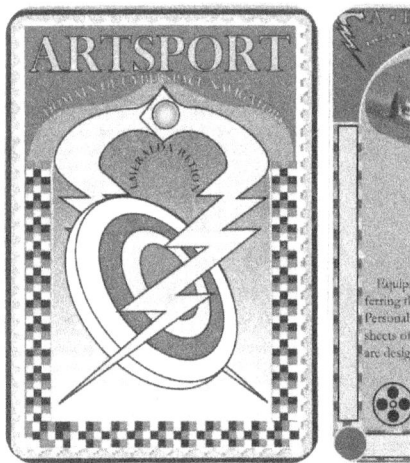
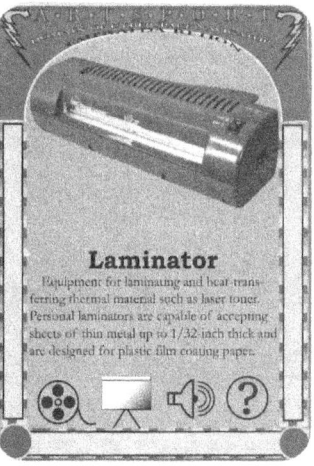

Figure 37: ArtsPort Resident Genius deck has sixteen cards, the ArtsPort deck has the ArtsPort banner on one side and the data on the other side.

17 ArtsPort Resident Genius

The front design resembles the Poster Deck No. 1 deck but the older one had a low-resolution image. This deck has ten *Printmaking Genius Tool* cards used in the studio of the Senior Artist in Residence, Professor Dustin "Dusty" Cann, the fictional, elusive missing professor in the Emeralda Adventure.

Professor Cann is the mentor whom the player seeks but with who he or she can never catch at work. These Genius Cards are prototypes for a combination tabletop game and interactive online story.

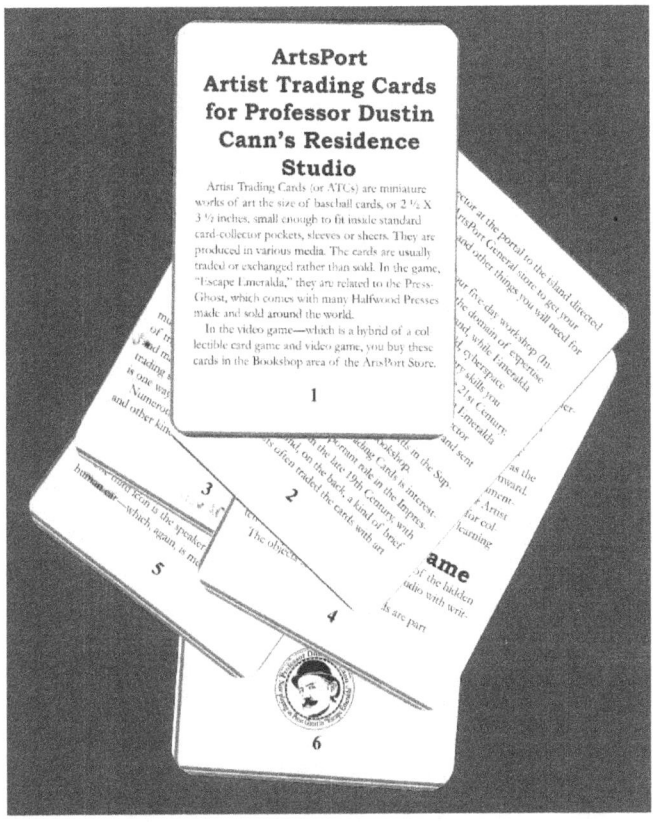

Figure 38: Six cards in this deck are given over to a brief explanation of Artist Trading Cards and an overview of the game mechanic.

The deck include six cards with the rules of the game printed on them—which were not yet completed and were thus unplayable at the time this deck was made.

Artists Collectible Trading Cards

In all there are one-hundred tools typically found in printmaking studios, from the ordinary roll of masking tape to the etching press itself. ArtsPort is the first of ten island a player encounters; and the ten tools on this deck (one being the laminator shown in the example above) are but the first of the tools the player collects and identifies.

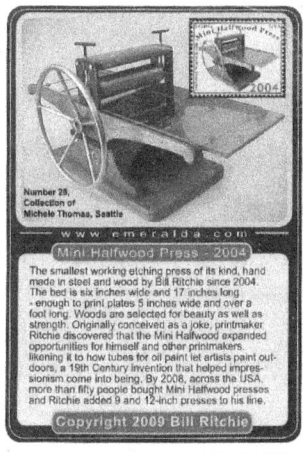 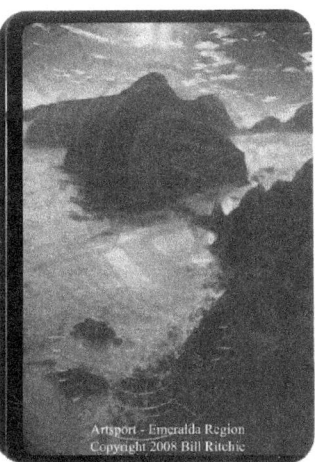

Figure 38: Mini Halfwood Press card four cards remain. It's unknown what quantity was made. These cards were given to most of the buyers of the original Legacy Mini Halfwood press from 2008 to 2010.

18 Mini Halfwood Press

Starting in 2004, I designed and built no fewer than five kinds of designer printmaking presses; and when I was exploring ways to promote games to teach how to use them online, I designed these cards to promote the presses.

This card is for the Legacy Mini Halfwood Press, similar in every way to the Galleon Halfwood Press cards (Number 11, above). Like the other card, it shows the image of *ArtsPort* referring to the mythical island in the legend of Emeralda—an

Artists Collectible Trading Cards

imaginary place where printmaking is the highest art form of intelligent use of resources.

The cards in this deck have been embossed with a hand-embosser, like a notary's, with the design of ArtsPort in it. It is one way to authenticate the card.

The image area is of course the Legacy Mini Halfwood Press, and a miniature stamp is placed in the upper corner. The text is written in third person (but of course I wrote the text):

> "The smallest working etching press of its kind, hand-made in steel and wood by Bill Ritchie since 2004. The bed is six inches wide an over a foot long. Woods are selected for beauty as well as strength. Originally conceived as a joke, printmaker Ritchie discovered that the Mini Halfwood expanded opportunities for himself and other printmakers, likening it to how tubes for oil paint let artists paint outdoors, a 19th Century invention that helped Impressionism come into being. By 2008, across the USA, more than fifty people bought Mini Halfwood Presses and Ritchie added 9 and 12-inch presses to his line."

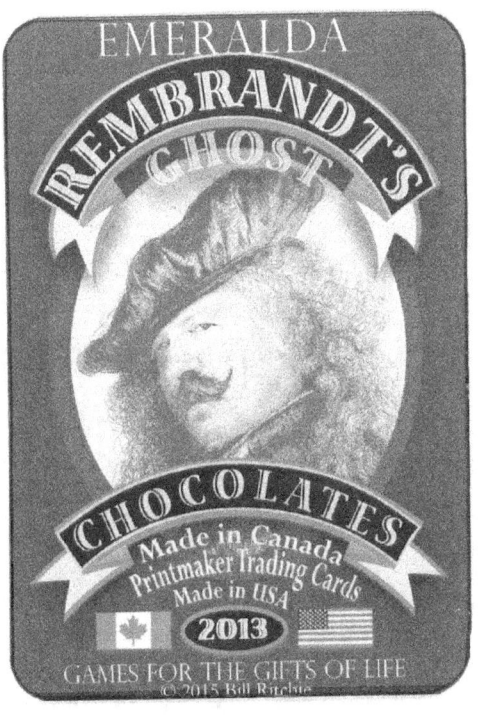

Figure 39: Rembrandt's Ghost Chocolates, the common side which backs all four of the cards in this deck.

19 Rembrandt's Ghost Chocolates

These were intended to go with Rembrandt's Chocolates, made in Canada by Ernest Horvers, who, with his wife, own the Rembrandt's Chocolate Company in Duncan, British Columbia. This episode in the Rembrandt's Ghost series began in 2012 with a letter to Ernest asking about formulating a chocolate that has the consistency of etching ink. As one might expect from a Dutch Master Chef and Chocolatier, this mystified him

What followed was a two-year series of experiments and give-and-take between this American artist and Ernest and his family. He showed me first that consistency was not an issue; he merely warmed the copper printing plate to print it. Even on a paper towel, it was convincing.

He used an electric frying pan, warmed the copper plate so that his "ink stick" (actually one of his signature, solid dark chocolates) melted. Then he wiped the plate in the normal way, warmed the copper again and printed it.

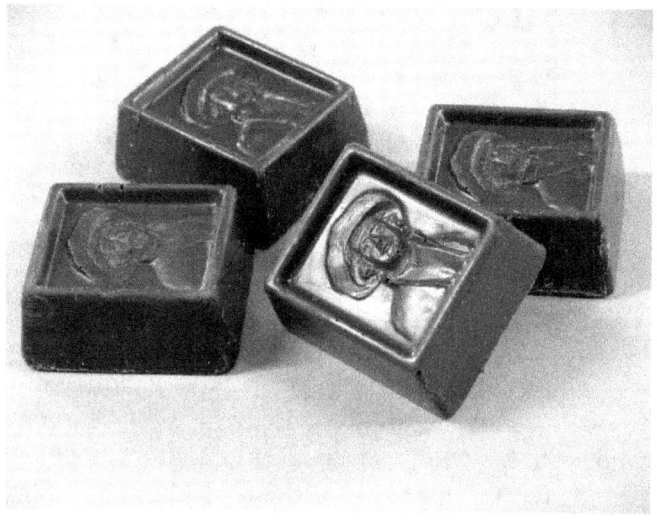

Figure 40: Rembrandt's chocolate, signature dark chocolate "ink blocks" Ernest used to print an etching.

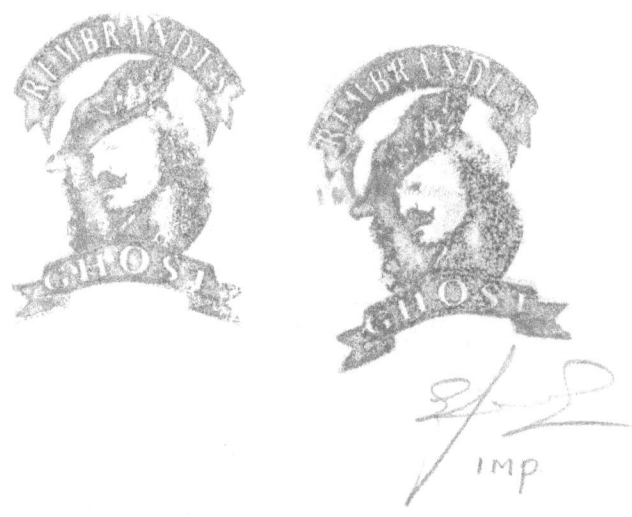

Figure 41: Chocolate printed on paper, Ernest Horvers' first experiment with printing from an etched copper plate using his dark chocolate as ink.

At this time Lynda and I were finishing the first edition of my novel, *Rembrandt's Ghost in the New Machine*, and for the Dutch speaking parts I used the computer translation. When Ernest saw these, he laughed and offered to correctly translate what the Dutch would really say, given Old Amsterdam colloquialisms and context.

We explored Rembrandt Chocolate bar labeling and chocolates packaged with Collectible Trading Cards, because I wanted to use the novel as back story to a game titled, *Mr. Rembrandt*.

Artists Collectible Trading Cards

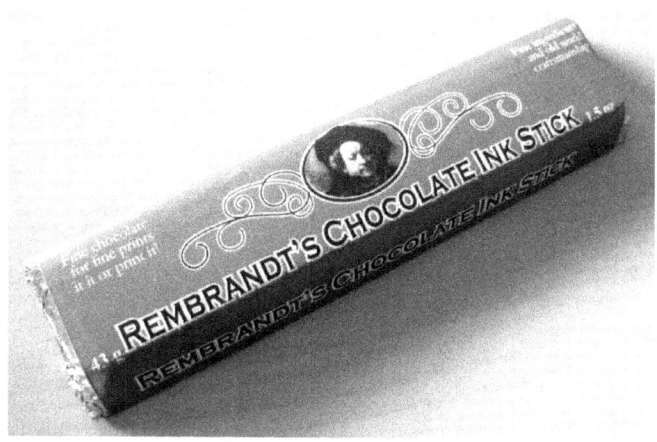

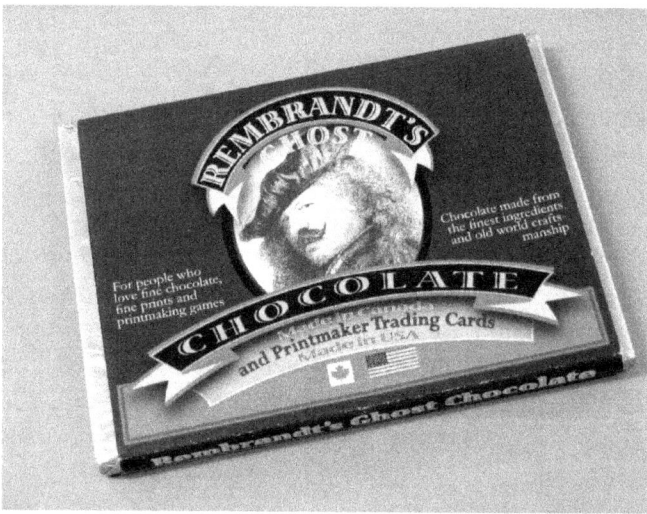

Figures 42, 43: Top, the Rembrandt's Chocolate bar wrapping design. We sold a couple dozen in Seattle at our coffee shop. Below, the flat bar design which was to have a trading card included in the package.

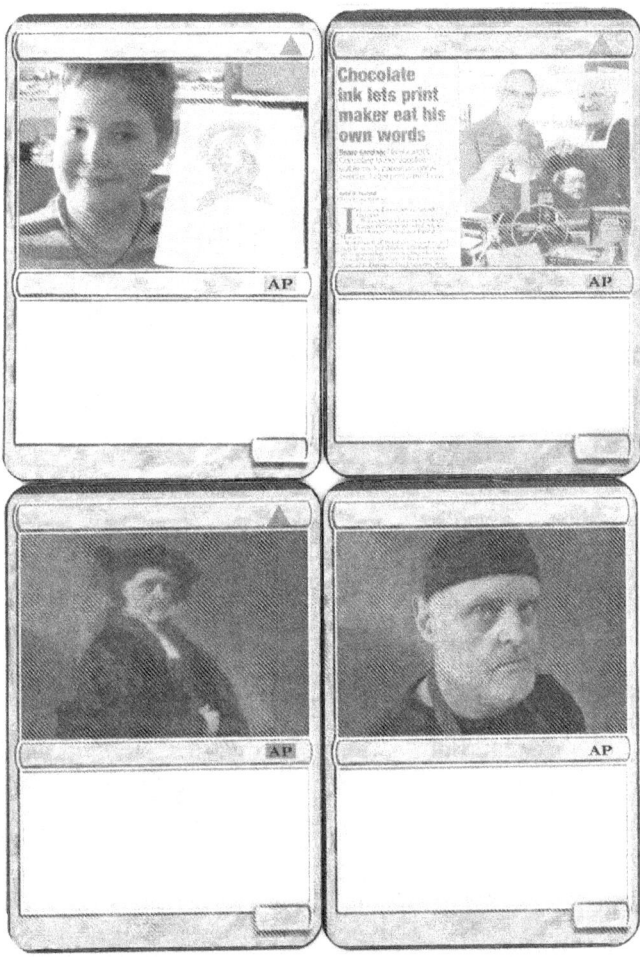

Figure 44: An unfinished trading card deck, the data sides. Upper left, Cory with his grandfather's chocolate print, a news article in Ernest's hometown announcing our book signing, and Ernest posing as Rembrandt.

Artists Collectible Trading Cards

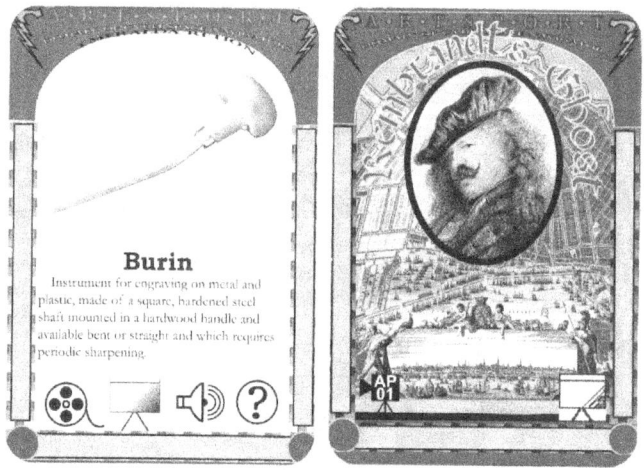

Figure 45: Rembrandt's Amsterdam, data side left, and common side, right.

20 Rembrandt's Amsterdam

The right image, above, shows the modified Rembrandt self-portrait superimposed over a map of 1660 Amsterdam, the setting for the novel, *Rembrandt's Ghost in the New Machine*. On the lower left corner the letters AP01 indicate a play in the proposed game, Rembrandt's Ghost, based on the novel. At the right corner, an old-style white projection screen. Other fields are blank, as this is a prototype for a deck for the game.

The screen, as well as a movie reel, speaker, and question mark line across the bottom, indicating resources which, if this were a virtual, interactive card, the player could access necessary information about the instrument shown—in this card, a square burin for engraving on metal.

There are sixteen cards in this deck. Ten are like the one above, with one of a hundred instrument, materials or supplies typically in a printmaking studio. Ten decks make up the suite, one for each island drawn from Eme*ralda Region*, an imaginary place.

This deck pre-dates the novel; the design was made concurrently with writing the chapters in the book so there is little or no connection between *Rembrandt's Ghost* … novel and *Emeralda Region*. Old Amsterdam, however, would serve as the world of the game, and Rembrandt's studio.

The remaining six cards have the rules (in tentative state, not playable in this deck) plus remarks about Artist Trading Cards. Following is the text on the six cards:

Rembrandt's Ghost
Artist Trading Cards

Artist Trading Cards (or ATCs) are miniature works of art the size of baseball cards, or 2 ½ X 3 ½ inches, small enough to fit inside standard card-collector pockets, sleeves or sheets. They are produced in various media. The cards are usually traded or exchanged rather than sold. In the game, "Rembrandt's Ghost," they are related to the PressGhost, a flash memory drive which comes with Rembrandt's WeeWoodie Etching Press.

In the game, Rembrandt's Ghost—which is a hybrid of a board game, collectible card game and video game, you buy these cards in the Bookshop area at the provisioners in the old city of Amsterdam where you must go to get your supplies, maps and other things you will need for your stay.

Artists Collectible Trading Cards

You know from your five-day workshop at Emeralda's Interval that ArtsPort is the imaginarium domain of expertise in cyberspace navigation, and, while Emeralda Region is a printmaking world, cyberspace navigation is one of the necessary skills you need if you are a printmaker in the 21st Century. The ferry that brought you here from Emeralda City Port left you at the docks of the old city of Amsterdam, the guards approached you, checked your identity, and sent you to the store. In the store, you find these cards in the Supplies section located near the Bookshop area.

The history of Artist Trading Cards is interesting. They played an important role in the Impressionists movement in the late 19th Century, with art on one side and, on the back, a kind of brief resume. Artists often traded the cards with art collectors in exchange for room, board, and art supplies. They were also used throughout Europe and America as art training tools. Artists would trade the cards among themselves to study each other's techniques and explore new art ideas and styles.

More recently, in 1996, M. Vänçi Stirnemann is credited with popularizing the modern Artist Trading Card, holding trading sessions in Zurich. Interest in Artist Trading Cards inspired copper plate cards which can be printed on an etching press to make ATCs. Clubs, trading sessions, and online mail art communities have largely replaced the original concept of trading the cards during individual encounters, and many ATC workshops and parties end with a trading session. On the Internet, www.meetup.com is one way of finding ATC groups nearby.

Numerous printmakers engage in making ATC and other kinds of miniature prints. This example is one Bill Ritchie makes for his series of games under the umbrella name, "Escape Emeralda." In this instance, the ATC is given the utility value as a collectible card—similar to the collectible cards in the games "Magic: The Gathering," "Pokémon," and "Bella Sera." Some cards have images on them that may be made into an etching plate and be printed, traded, sold or altered, as Artist Trading Cards are free of restrictions and intended for learning—just as the original cards served in the 19th Century onward. At the time of this writing, Bill is experimenting with a game involving these as copper Artist Trading Cards, and as such they may be for collecting and entertainment blended with learning printmaking.

Rules of the Game
The objects shown in these cards are part of a modern day printmaking studio--far, far ahead of Rembrandt's time. In the PressGhost you find the game that goes with these cards. You can find the objects in the image, click on them, and it will open the digital version of this card, and you notice in the image (as you do in the real card) icons that show (1) a video camera, (2) a slide screen, (3) a speaker and (4) a question mark.

The video camera on the paper version of the card can do nothing, of course, because it is in the perfect, analog information world—it cannot be changed. On the computer screen, however, it's in the imperfect world and it can change if you click on it. Clicking on the movie reel will bring a movie about the object to the screen. One example is the showman, Dusty Cann, in a blue wig and bowler hat explaining the above ten objects in a modern printmaking studio. (Rembrandt would be astounded if he knew--like the movie, *Kate and Leopold*.) The slide icon, too, is unchangeable on the card; but in the digital card, clicking on it will changed it to a slide presentation about the object—the familiar PowerPoint presentation.

The third icon is the speaker which, again, is merely a suggestion on the paper-based card but when clicked on the computer screen, gives you the spoken name of the object. English is one version, but in localized versions it can be in other languages. Or, if you are an ESL player, you might want only the English version. Some printmaking objects have kept the name given to them by printmakers in other countries. Japanese woodblock printmaking, for example, gives you the Japanese pronunciation.

Finally, the question mark; honestly, the designer of this game didn't know what to put in the fourth icon's place. It could be a link to a search engine that would take you to a Web site; for example, Wikipedia would be one possibility. Think of it like a link to Google, a very popular source of information both educational and commercial.

Artists Collectible Trading Cards

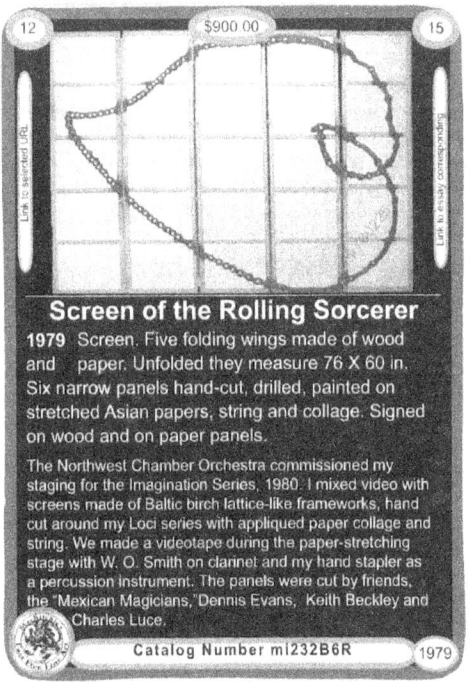

Figure 46: Screen of the Rolling Sorcerer, one of six cards in this deck, so named because the card for this artwork happened to be on the top.

21 Screen of the Rolling Sorcerer

This Artist's Collectible Trading Card is based on one of the six folding screens commissioned by the Northwest Chamber Orchestra and sold to collectors in the 1980s. Titled, *Screen of the Rolling Sorcerer*, this card is one of six cards in the deck of a certain design for several proposed uses: (1) as labels for works on display, (2) as trading cards and, (3) as digital collectible trading cards.

The artwork associated with this card is owned by a collector named David Prentice but it is stored at the Ritchie family's Mini Art Gallery at the time of this writing. Nellie Sunderland, asset manager for the Ritchie Family, customized a fabric liner for its box; I made the box for this screen. At this time there has been no word from David Prentice regarding its disposition.

The card is one of six representative designs for this ACTC deck showing the influence from the collectible trading card games of the 1990s. Earlier I had designed cards using Excel spreadsheet software (shown in a later chapter, Number 27, below).

The other five designs are for five other items in the Ritchie Family Collection consisting of ceramics, prints, ephemera and mixed media works. The layouts are the same, but some fields have not been populated.

For example, one card has an essay number printed in a field, referring to one of my thousands of essays and which I wrote approximately at the time I made the art: os060726. This number, when entered into a search window on my system (or, a database on the cloud or an eBook version, game, etc.) would yield the essay.

Artists Collectible Trading Cards

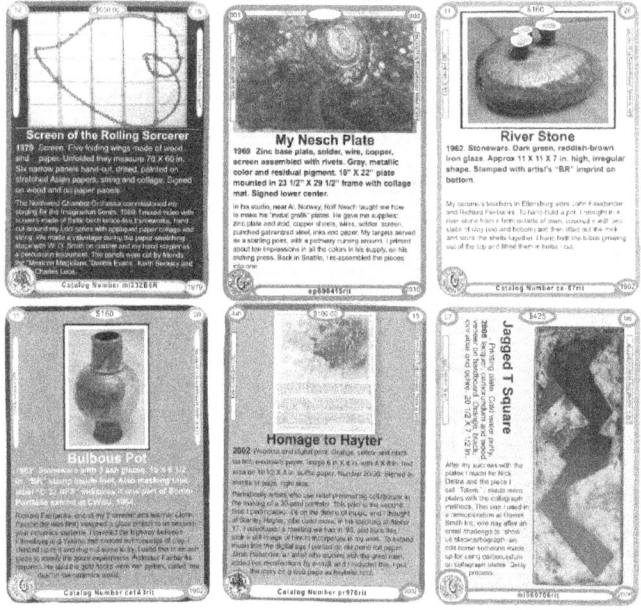

Figure 47: The six cards that make up the deck, Screen of the Rolling Sorcerer (upper left card) deck.

The layout is that of many collectible trading cards. A schema of nine cells contain a picture of the artwork, text describing it (also known as the provenance and back story) plus fields which might be used to contain hyperlinks, QR codes or similar data to extend the functionality of the cards in either physical or digital forms.

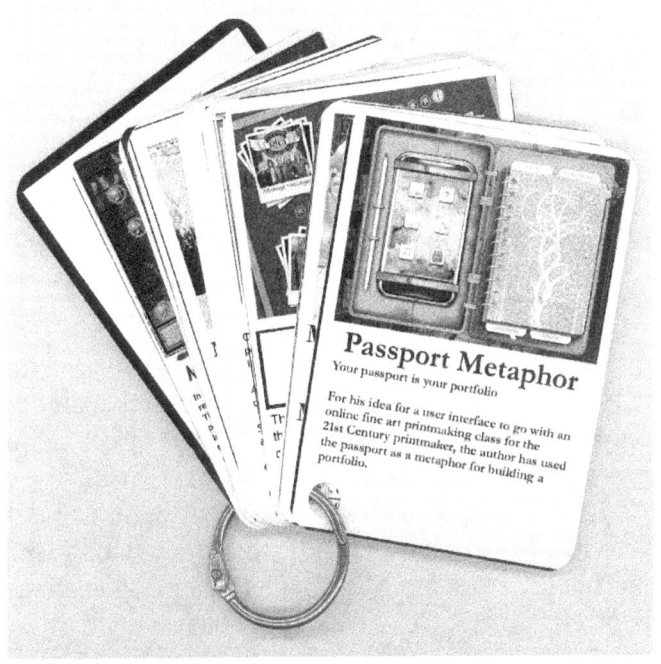

Figure 48: Passport Metaphor, the deck named for the card which happened to be on the top of the display, but there are 23 cards in all based on a gamified CD produced by the band, REO Speedwagon.

22 Passport Metaphor

Writing for the graphic novel and cards for *Printmaking Camp*, there was an advergame by a rock group, REO Speedwagon, which served as a metaphor. I took screenshots of their designs and wrote my own version of how I would design for my game to teach printmaking methods on the web.

Artists Collectible Trading Cards

There are twenty-three cards with a hole punched in the corner and held together by a key ring. There is no order in which they are attached—just random images and random thoughts about adapting this interactive game in my plans.

At the time I was working with this metaphor, I was also working on a narrative titled *Printmaking Camp*, which has possibilities for a ten-part advergame or serial television program.

The script for *Printmaking Camp* is an extension of my screen play, *Swipe*, and includes one of the main characters—an adopted street kid, a girl named "Issey" (and sometimes Issy, with no *e*). As I was using with the REO Speedwagon game it was helpful to show myself how a suite of game mechanics—Hidden Object Games, puzzles, first-person-shooters, etc.—could populate a single title.

Also, the art for the game—drawn by Nellie Sunderland using Manga Studio software—was influenced by the black-and-white drawings they used in the REO Speedwagon game. In the figure below, one panel shows the ringed deck of cards and, in the selected lines from the script, reads the line from the screenplay. The deck of collectible trading cards, the story line of *Printmaking Camp*, and the graphic novel of all ten episodes is a three-part plan.

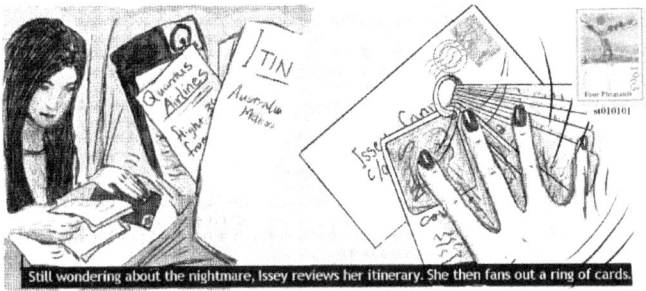

INT. PLANE - DAY

Ah! ISSEY wakens. Eyes wide. It was just a bad dream, but so realistic it makes her wonder. Oh well. Relax.

CLOSEUP

She takes her itinerary from her bag. We note the first stop: AUSTRALIA. Now she takes out ART CARDS ON A RING and fans out the cards on her serving tray. She fixes on one.

Figure 49: Panel and script from the graphic novel, *Printmaking Camp*, which parallels the development of screenplay, graphic novel, and collectible trading cards.

The bottom of the frame shown above is from the first, opening installment of the storyboard from *Printmaking Camp* and it shows how my plan of collectible card decks is interwoven (recursive) with two other works—graphic novel and TV serial.

Artists Collectible Trading Cards

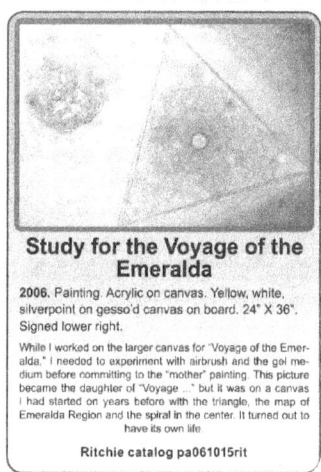

Figure 50: Study for the Voyage of the Emeralda, the top card of a sample deck designed to be giving away to visitors to the Ritchie Family Mini Art Gallery for sales promotion.

23 Study for the Voyage of the Emeralda

The artwork for this card, which is part of a deck of promotional cards, is a painting made concurrently with the larger painting, *Voyage of the Emeralda*, commissioned by Nick Dellos. Nick is a designer and was at work on a downtown Seattle penthouse. He wanted art for his project and I made three—including the large *Voyage*—and this canvas was a practice piece for it.

This deck is similar to other decks that are based on my works of art, having an image, text, and provenance data. It should be mentioned that many of my works—about 400 or more—are catalogued in Microsoft Access database, which facilitates including provenance data.

> **Study for the Voyage of the Emeralda**
>
> **2006.** Painting. Acrylic on canvas. Yellow, white, silverpoint on gesso'd canvas on board. 24" X 36". Signed lower right.
>
> While I worked on the larger canvas for "Voyage of the Emeralda," I needed to experiment with airbrush and the gel medium before committing to the "mother" painting. This picture became the daughter of "Voyage ..." but it was on a canvas I had started on years before with the triangle, the map of Emeralda Region and the spiral in the center. It turned out to have its own life.
>
> **Ritchie catalog pa061015rit**

Figure 51: A close up of the data on the sample card shows the extent of provenance for this artwork.

The database itself is extensible; that is, digital versions of collectible trading card games can be realized more effectively if data about the art is in an Extensible Markup Language (XML) form.

Artists Collectible Trading Cards

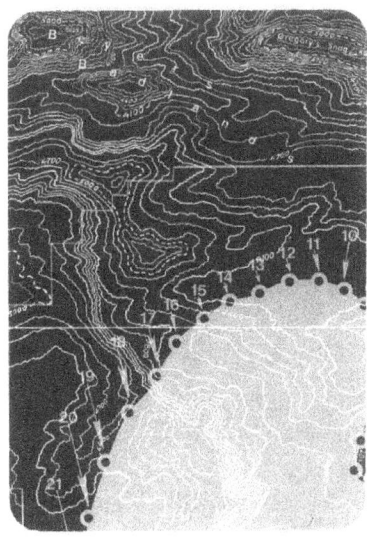

Figure 52: Cyanotype Poster Cut-up, one of twenty-four cards cut from a ten-by-fourteen inch print which is reduced image of the original 24-by-40 inch 1982 poster, *Cyanotype Commemorative*.

24 Cyanotype Poster Cut-up

Assembly of these cards makes the complete image of the cyanotype poster image area, but in less than half the actual size. Twenty-four cards make the deck. The original is a six-color print.

Although the 1982 poster was an offset lithograph, I made hand-drawn masters to make the plates—not photography. To create the blended colors I worked with the plate maker, the printer and I also mixed the inks.

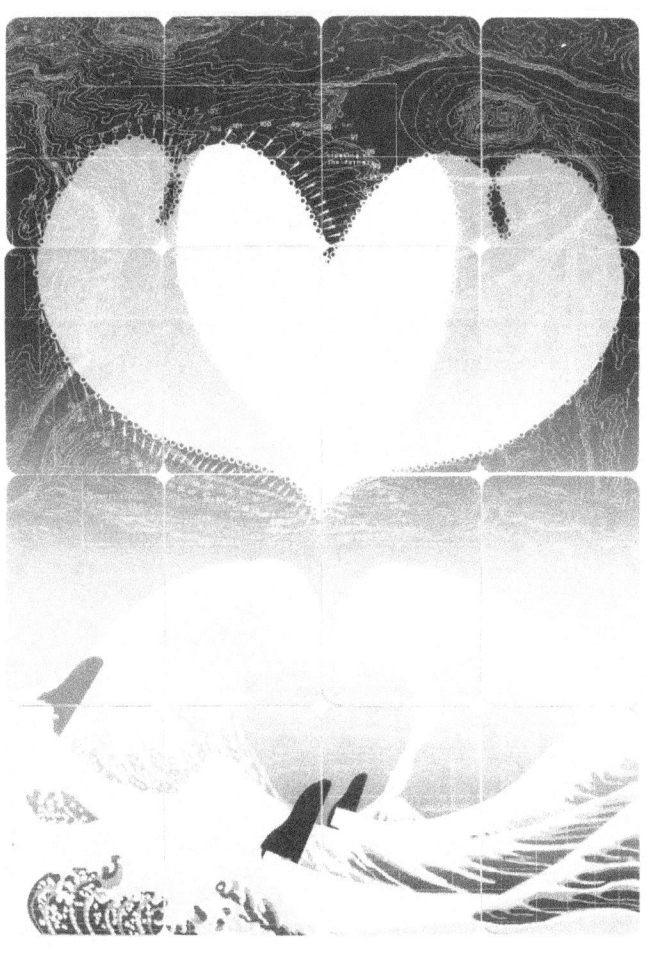

Figure 53: The tones of blue were overprinted with transparent gloss yellow inks on 165 lb. Warren Patina pH Neutral paper. The actual poster, including the text, measures 40 X 24 3/4 in. Eleven hundred were printed, of which I recycled 850—keeping back a few hundred.

Artists Collectible Trading Cards

The influences on me were cartography, computer technology and Japanese culture from three sources: (1) A map of the Colorado River, Lake Powell area, (2) a leaf-like pattern in hand-cut copper (which I also used for computer animation) and (3) the famous woodblock print by Hokusai titled popularly-known as *The Great Wave*. For the land features I used the names of my family and studio mates, producing a fantasy map based on the region in Arizona.

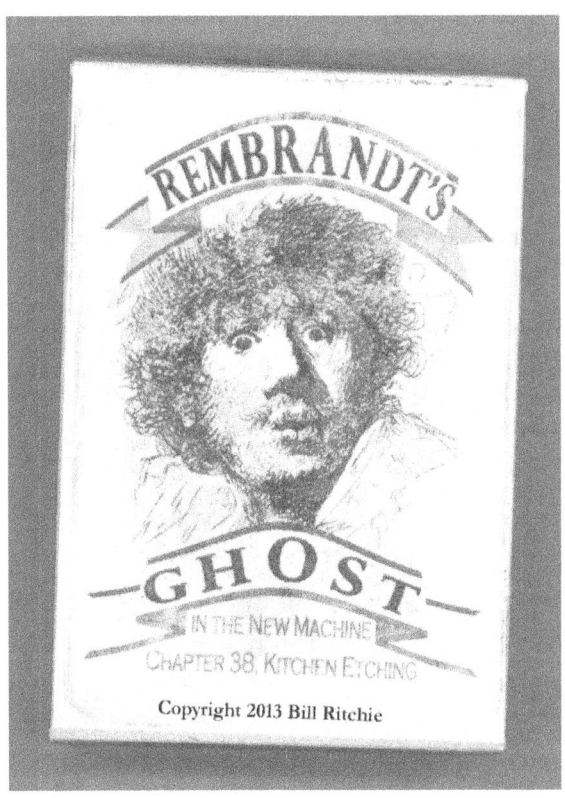

Figure 54: Kitchen Etching, the front cover of the box containing a paper trial proof of the deck.

25 Kitchen Etching

I intended my 2013 novel, *Rembrandt's Ghost in the New Machine* as the back story for a collectible trading card game, and this box for a trial proof copy of the deck represents Chapter 38 of the novel's 2nd edition.

Artists Collectible Trading Cards

The deck box design features Chapter 38 because of the easily recognized self-portrait by Rembrandt titled *Self Portrait with a Cap*. It is one that was made for designing graphics and text for the box prior to trying out a box-making service online called *Gamecrafters*. There are fifty four cards in the deck.

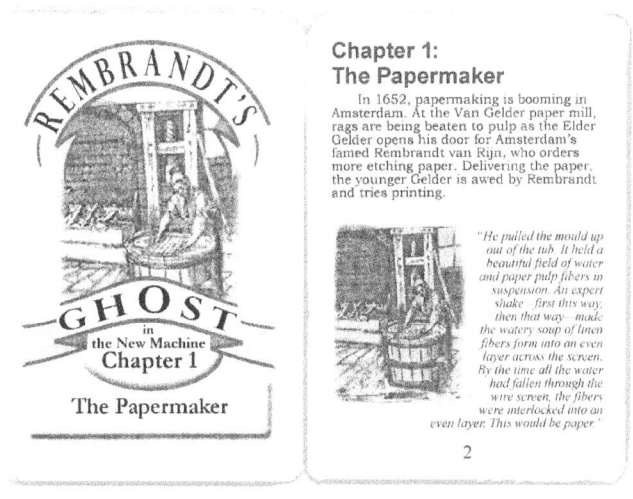

Figure 55: The fifty-four cards in the deck represent all the cards in the deck. This illustration shows the image side and the text side.

Each card has two sides—an image side and a story side. The same image is inserted in both sides. The illustration shows the card for Chapter 1, The Papermaker. The text side has two fields following the title. The first field is a 50-word summary of the entire chapter. The second field is a word-for-word extract from the chapter, a sentence or two chosen to give the player an impression of the writing style. The number at the bottom of the card happens to belong to a miniature book, it is page two from the mini book version of *Rembrandt's Ghost in the New Machine*.

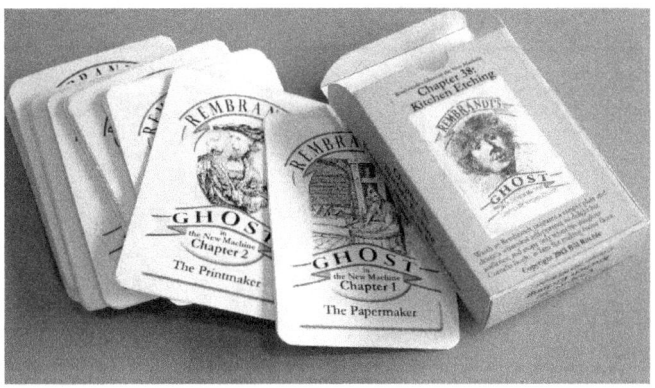

Figure 56: The box for the cards for *Rembrandt's Ghost – The card game*, and its contents.

Artists Collectible Trading Cards

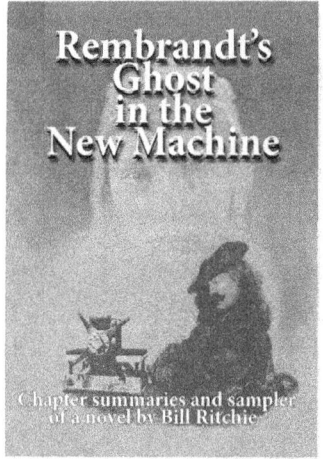

Figure 57: Rembrandt's Ghost Covers is an anomaly where trading cards are concerned because it is a deck of four cards showing front and back and inside the covers of the mini-book version of the novel.

26 Rembrandt's Ghost Covers

Four cards made of the covers for the Minibook sampler for my novel, *Rembrandt's Ghost in the New Machine*. This is one of my experiments in which I am search for links among storytelling, collectible cards, board games and printmaking. The illustration above is the front cover and inside the front.

Miniature books always fascinate me, and I made miniature version of the novel, giving a single, card-sized page to each chapter in the novel. The covers of the mini-books were printed on heavyweight glossy stock, and the inside pages were printed in four signatures and perfect-bound so they could be glued inside the covers. The books fit in a shirt pocket and they also would fit inside a card deck box.

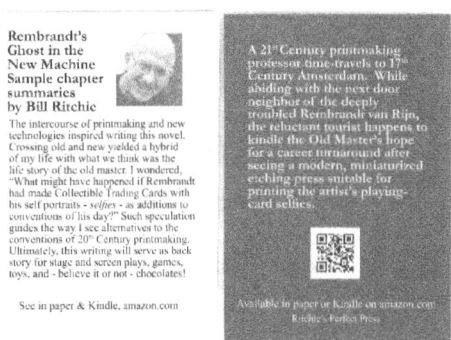

Figure 58: Back cover of the mini-book and the inside of the back cover.

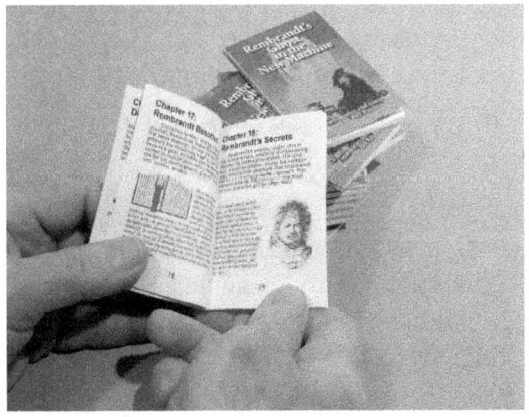

Figure 59: The miniature version of the novel

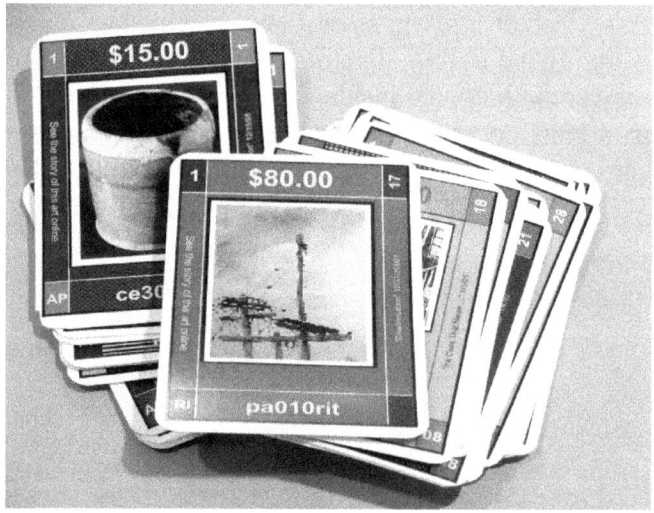

Figure 60: Emeralda Games, first deck.

27 Emeralda Games

The first card concept for *Emeralda*, my *Games for the Gifts of Life*. It was in the year 1998 when I assumed that the cards would be a hybrid blend of physical cards and digital cards playable on the web or other platforms—including the Halfwood and Wee Woodie Rembrandt presses.

It was my assumption that the design must be in Extensible Markup Language (XML) and the cards would have hotspots and link the user to more data, images, videos, etc. Therefore I used Microsoft Excel spreadsheet software to design the card, with nine cells for the face of the card and one for the back (ten cells total) and assigned images, text and numbers for each cell. Following this I used Microsoft Access to inventory my artworks with an indexing system to facilitate searches.

In my videos, *Emeralda Inventor Interviews*, viewers can detect that I did not yet have the design or game mechanic finished. Admittedly, *Emeralda* is a never-ending game, although when my life is over, my hope is that it may be playable and be a benefit to Emeralda players.

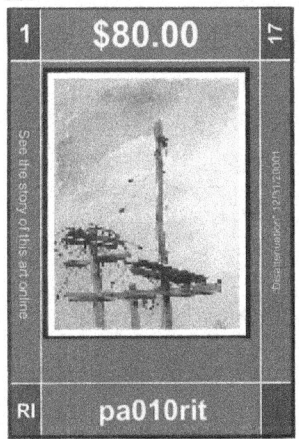 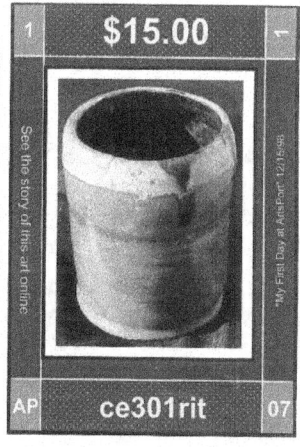

Figure 61: Two selections from the deck, pictured in the figure above, showing some details of the cards.

The two letters at the lower left corner indicate on which of the ten imaginary islands in *Emeralda Region* (the parallel universe I set up in the early 1990s) this card is played.

Artists Collectible Trading Cards

In this basic card design (which showed only the image side, or cells 1-9), the example at the left of power poles has the index name pa010rit at the bottom. Its provenance in the Access, says:

> **Catalog Number: pa010rit Title: Power Pole. 1963**. Watercolor. Blue, browns, black. Image bleeds to edge of 22 X 15 in. watercolor paper. Signed lower right.
> **Artist's statement:** "When I had my paints in hand and a new sheet of watercolor stretched and ready to go, it seemed like everything and anything qualified for a good subject to paint. Even a power pole against the windblown cloudy autumn sky of the Kittitas Valley was beautiful, and I loved it! My teachers, Paul Heald and Ron Carraher, by turns, helped turn me on to watercolor--but I came back to printmaking in the end."
> **Valuation:** Cost of goods: $16.00. Current value: $128.00. Reserve: $80.00. Date acquired: October 15, 1963.

In the Access database for the card on the right, with the index name ce301rit, reads:

> **Catalog Number: ce301rit. Title: Cylinder #1. 1960.** Ceramic. Mid-fired with three glazes. Celadon, white, transparent colors. 5 1/2 in. high, 3 1/2 in. diameter. Inscribed on bottom "1960 Bill Ritchie".
> **Artist's statement:** "I consider myself lucky because I enrolled for pre-professional (or portfolio preparation) for Art Center School in California and therefore I was able to jump right into my art courses in my freshman year, taking ceramics. My teacher, John Fassbinder, taught me to use the wheel. This is my first cylinder, glazed with the pot-shop's supply of communal glazes."
> **Valuation:** Cost of goods: $10.00. Current value: $100.00. Reserve: $25.00. Date acquired: Nov. 15, 1960.

In addition to my graphics, I love to write essays on ideas that come to me in the course of my work and since I first began using computers in 1979, I made use of word processors and text editors and mapped them according to a timetable plus an indexing system based on the ten islands of *Emeralda Region*, plus one directory called *Interval*.

In one cell, on the right edge, I place the index number of an essay in the library of 'Zines on any of the *Domains-of-Expertise*—the islands. It should be mentioned here that I have notions of teaching for people who like to read, as most essays are from 500-1500 words. The card at the right in the examples shows the essay is, *My first day at ArtsPort*, dated 12/15/98, and the comment line for which reads:

> ap981215: My First Day at ArtsPort: The third year of living copiously. The author, formerly with a university teaching art courses, compares one manager of a mutual fund in securities with college class management. He wonders whether the comparison of students to customers has validity when he encounters his former students. ©1998 Bill H Ritchie

Anyone wishing to read this essay in 1998 might have done so by email request but today it would by searching on the cloud using the number, ap981215. Interestingly, proving this at the time of this writing, Google's search engine yields an article with the same alphanumeric index on a website called *Learn Astronomy*, associated with an article by Robert J. Nemiroff, an Astrophysicist at Michigan Technological University and NASA Goddard.

An alternative I use is a QR (Quick Response) code, as seen on other decks and shown in earlier chapters. For this book, the QR code is an add-on for demonstration; it was not on the original 1998 cards. QR code was invented in 1994 by a Toyota subsidiary for manufacturing. Twenty years later I adopted QR codes when I had a smartphone.

Artists Collectible Trading Cards

Figure 62: Variation on the cards, this one having provenance text printed on the verso of the card. The QR code is a much later version than the original, the original dating before the year 2000 and QR codes were unknown.

QR codes are used today in everything from inventory tracking, shipping, logistics, and online ticketing. Artists put them on art labels to link to their websites or get subscribers to their social network pages. Businesses use it to put Google Maps directions on a business card, automatically load a web page, or send a text/email to the company helpline. A wildlife refuge in Florida installed the codes on signs along hiking trails and linked them to information about the local fauna you can access on a mobile.

The main impetus driving me in making trading cards based on my art is to extend the experience—the creative process, the techniques, the back story, and knowing the people who share ownership or in other ways experience my art. Adding a QR code enables today's users to participate in ways that were unimaginable before technologies like the Internet and QR codes.

For example, two people own the artwork in Figure 62, and many of my art patrons (also owners of the Halfwood Press line I designed) have a page on my websites, these two included. With the card in hand, a user can scan the QR code and their device will show those art owners' pages. My brief back story about our relationship is included, as well as the provenance and an image. Sometimes the owner has a website, and a link is given.

For owners of more than one artwork, the user may find those, also; these artworks, in turn, may be owned in other collections, with more back stories, more links and, occasionally, videos.

This is a different kind of collectible card game proposition, where artists' legacies, translated into games (gamified) might reach a new level. Just as the art world is sometimes referred to as *the art game*, and in the same way that Extensible Markup Language (XML) in software design extends the functionality of software, artworks may find a new life and new audiences if the artist permits.

Artists Collectible Trading Cards

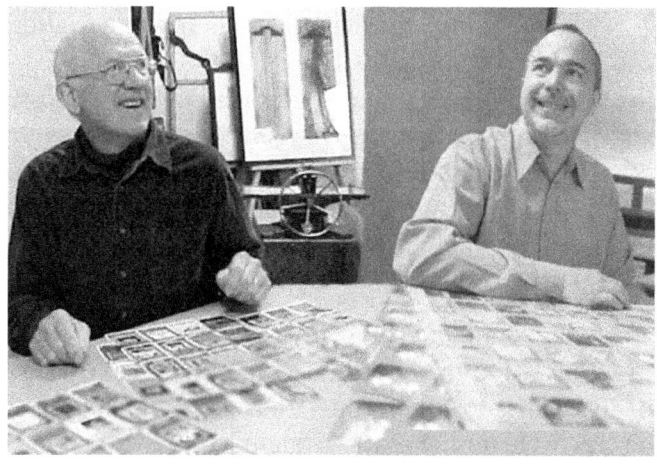

Figure 63: Me, left, posing with my cards, about 1999. Enamored of *Magic: The Gathering* cards, and I saw Peter Adkison's photo on the web, and I altered it as a joke photo of myself in the same pose with my cards.

My aim as an artist has always been to make effective art. As a kid I was influenced by media art—printing, movies, TV—that could reach far out into the hinterlands of my childhood. If artists can do that with media, then the language of the mediums of video, games, and collectible cards can be effective, too.

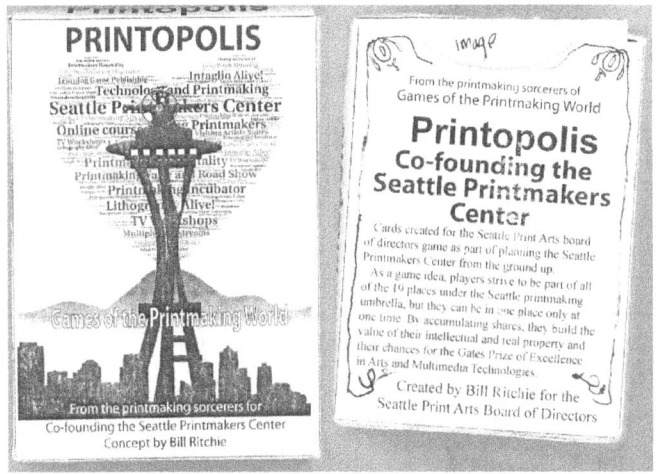

Figure 64: Printopolis box for the cards, proposed design for the front (left) and back in its original black-and-white, a sketch version. The text on the back of the box can be read below.

28 Printopolis

In 2014, the first year of planning the Northwest Print Center & Incubators (the name of which had changed from the original as seen in the box image in figure 64), the online gamification course would come in handy. A collectible card game would be an appropriate use of what I learned in my gamification class—a Massively Open Online Course (MOOC) from the Wharton School of Business at the University of Pennsylvania.

For my card game's first iteration, made in January of 2015, I time it for a scheduled

Artists Collectible Trading Cards

presentation to the Board of Directors of the *Seattle Print Arts,* Seattle's only printmakers' club. I was advised to ask the SPA about teaming up, in co-founding and extending printmaking toward a *Seattle Printmakers Center.* I brought a rack card for reference and my card deck. The text on the back of the card box reads:

> From the printmaking sorcerers for Games of the Printmaking World
> Co-founding the Seattle Printmakers Center
> Cards created for the Seattle Print Arts Board of Directors, a game as part of planning the Seattle Printmakers Center from the ground up.   As a game idea, players strive to be part of all of the 19 places under the Seattle printmaking umbrella, but they can be in one place only at one time. By accumulating shares, they build the value of their intellectual and real property and their chances for the Gates Prize of Excellence in Arts and Multimedia Technologies.
> Created by Bill Ritchie for
> the─────────────────Seattle Print Arts Board of Directors

At the meeting in February I passed out the cards in the deck to the dozen members assembled for their annual meeting and asked them for questions. After the Q&A, their consensus of opinion was that I should to go on with my plan without them, on my own, and not compete with their mission.

The SPA mission is: "... *to foster intellectual and artistic dialogue, serve as a resource for news in the field of printmaking, forge links between artists, and serve as a base for a variety of activities that focus on the print arts.*"

Since that time I had opportunities to study ways to play this game beyond the purpose for which it was made. I have yet to come up with a game mechanic or method of play, but here is my first attempt:

> The object of Printopolis is to overcome insurmountable obstacles and win the Gates Prize and select a preferred Domain-of-Expertise in Northwest Print Center Incubators. There are nineteen domains, every one different but interdependent on the others. You may be a winner in more than one place, but only at one time can you be resident in one place.
> In this iteration, five players take the roles of Artist, Printer, Preparator, Publisher and Collector. The winner of the game wins the Gates Prize - Year of Living Copiously in the paradisiacal Emeralda Region. While this may sound wonderful, but you must be aware that there dangerous Wizards of Awe waiting to smother your creative fire.
> Begin your role playing by rolling dice. The player with the highest number is first to choose their preferred role. They take the badge of their role. Ties are replayed, the higher number taking turns in choosing roles.

Play begins with the first player rolling the dice and advancing their badge that many squares. The instructions on their landing indicates the action to be taken, and in accordance with the player's role.

The reader will detect several mysterious references: *Gates Prize, A Year of Living Copiously*, and *Emeralda Region*. Also, terms like *Artist*, *Printer*, *Preparator*, *Publisher* and *Collector* may have obvious meaning, yet how they interact with other players is undefined.

The mysteries are unintended, and in other writings I have expanded on the terms in great detail—probably too great detail! Frankly, I feel as though I am exercising the same creative license

Artists Collectible Trading Cards

that game inventors, fantasy fiction authors and storytellers have used throughout history.

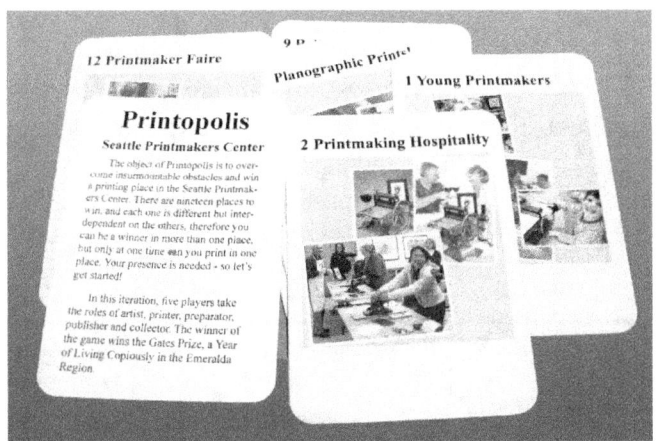

Figure 65: Samples of the nineteen game cards made for the first iteration of a proposal to "gamify" the planning and development of the Northwest Print Center & Incubators.

29 Conclusion to Part I

This book has no ending in sight. I can only conclude there is no conclusion—as games are, in their best form, endlessly played and varied according to the times and the people who use them for play, for learning, and power.

Part II
Fantasy printmaking trading card games

Preface to Part II

The objective of all Emeralda Trading Card Games (TCG) is to destroy the Ominium Gatherum and all the evils for which he stands. Beware of the Omnium Gatherum! For human life, this is important, because the Omnium Gatherum wants to smother all human life in carbon dioxide. They who struggle to reverse the deadly buildup of carbon dioxide become eligible for the Gates Prize, and they are known as Emeralda Warriors.

Gates Prize defined

No printmaking experience is complete without the hope for winning a Gates Prize; but, you may wonder, "What is the Gates Prize?" It's a prize of the imagination, like the pot of gold at the end of a rainbow. Although the Gates Prize is imaginary, it is still a prize worthy of your striving if you are a teacher or a student and a member of a team of teachers and students acting to save Earth's Human Life Sustainability.

The Gates Prize is awarded to individuals and teams who demonstrate awesome achievements in teaching, research, practice and service to humanity. Teachers, especially, dream of winning the prize because if they do win, their reward is a year in Emeralda Region—the haven for all the things teachers dream of and, sometimes, they still achieve in the real world.

The Gates Prize came from the concept of "The World Teachers," which was introduced in the biography of Elmer Gates, who was born in 1856 and was a pioneering researcher in learning and brain development. You might compare him to Jules Verne, who inspired Steampunk. Gates used himself as a guinea pig, going to extremes like shutting himself in a room to see if sensory deprivation would aid him in solving problems and inventing machines and discovering how to get gold out of sand. His biography, "Elmer Gates and the Art of Mind Using," written by one of his sons, Donald. This book, and his records in the Smithsonian Library, are the few remaining artifacts of his genius and his inventive life.

The Gates Prize referred to in Emeralda ATC never existed in the real world, although Elmer D. Gates, carries on the educational mission of the name through the organization, *SkillsUSA Council*, which awards prizes to outstanding students in the Allentown, Pennsylvania area. Perhaps he is another son, or grandson, of Elmer Gates.

Gates' vision and others

Other visionaries besides Elmer Gates, like Vannevar Bush, Albert Einstein, and H. G. Wells were born in the late 1800s and documented their vision of a great, all-encompassing library or depository that would bring world peace and prosperity for all people. Their writings include references to, "The next hundred years." Now it is time to review what they said. How are we doing? Can we test what they forecast, and consider what lies ahead?

Central to this vision is education for all—not necessarily the kind of education we know from our past hundred years' of United States history, but an advanced kind of education, the principles of which we, as a species, have been unable to achieve.

Today, we can think of the Internet and World Wide Web as the fulfillment of these visionaries' ideas. After a quarter century since the Web was released and browser software was written for regular people, has it fulfilled the vision? Is there progress? Could it be the Web has made Earth's sustainability of the human species *less* likely? Imagine if technology had got stuck somewhere early last century instead?

Consider Steampunk in William Gibson's book, "The Difference Engine," and what could have happened and—for some people—what *is* happening.

Now consider the role of all the arts in this context—the forms of art that can, and are, translated into machine language that can flash over the Web. Many people believe that Web-based games are the art of the 21st Century, and this book agrees.

Introduction – On speculation

Writing this book is speculative, like launching a ship with a captain, navigator and crew—and not one among them is certain of the destination; and, worse, no one knows how to get there. As game designers, we build our road as we travel it. We play our way toward our destination—which is to conserve Earth's Human Life Sustainability for as long as we have a chance, using digital devices to make and play analog card games—using past experience and intuition as our guides.

Rulebook or textbook?

Games that already exist have rules. Games that are speculative have no published rules at first. Rules are like laws—in human societies, laws evolved as they were needed to achieve goals. Peace, for example, is a goal which is basic to laws. To live is another, basic goal. Many of life's goals are unconscious; at times, such as near death, the simplest goal—to live—may leap into clear view and then we act with vigor and all the strength we have.

Other times, goals lie quietly in the back of our mind, barely noticed. It is only by an act of conscious planning and action do we make goals real and within our grasp. When we write down a goal on a piece of paper—or on the mirror where we will be reminded of it when we start our day—we achieve progress toward our goals.

Games offer lessons in goals. Games that require strategic thinking teach lessons very well. Chess is a supreme example. Games that require luck also have lessons to offer—that setting a goal is not enough. You have to have luck on your side, too.

This book is not as much a rule book that explains how to play the Ten Emeralda Collectible Trading Card Games as it is a textbook for online courses. Not just any online course; only fine art printmaking courses. Understanding how a published book—that which you are holding in your hand if you have the paper version or an eBook or seeing on your eBook reader—can be tentative requires living in the age of digital reproduction.

Breaking ground by breaking rules

The age of digital reproduction makes publishing books different than it was in the age of mechanical reproduction. This goes for textbooks, too, such as this one. To learn fine art printmaking—which is the goal of all students in Emeralda, the new school of printmaking—you must see this kind of printmaking is based on the fact that rules are made to be tested and, sometimes, broken.

Online TCGs, time and space

If there are online versions of the games included in this book, it may be possible that you can interact with the person closest to you on the Printmaking World Map of the Earth.

This printmaker is a "Proximate," i.e., you found them using their Kyber Etching press at almost the same time as you were using your Kyber Press.

Foreword - Thanks to former students

It is frequently said by teachers that they learn from their students. It is frequently true, and in my case, I can testify in detail what I learned from my former students. Plus, as I am a lifelong teacher and learner, I am continuing to learn from other people although we may not be in a conscious teacher/student relationship.

What I learned from my students and why these facts are in this foreword to a textbook on fantasy printmaking trading card games owes mainly to my career as a college professor from 1966-1985. My campus career began in a strange way and ended, also, strangely.

It was not a remarkable beginning on the surface: the University of Washington School Of Art needed another faculty member to teach printmaking, and I was hired. But underneath this unremarkable beginning of my career there were factors working about which I learned little by little and—after nineteen years—ended in rejection from the institution. When I look back, it was like an escape from a prison. This probably shaped my thinking about games that have a purpose.

The beginnings were remarkable in a second factor in that I spent my fall quarter commuting between the Business School and the School of Art. The art building had no office space when I started my first term, so I got an office in the Business School. That turned out to be important. Right away, I had an outsider's view—from a business window as it were, literally and figuratively—of the business of art.

During those years it was the students who taught me what I needed to know to be a lifelong teacher and learner in the arts, equivalent to post-doctorate studies but with a salary and tenure.

It wasn't conscious on either of our parts; they didn't always know what they were doing, and, much of the time, neither did I. We went through the motions, trying this, that and the other thing, like a herd of cats in a maze. End the end, while never intending to, I created alternative printmaking teaching—almost reinvented it.

When I left the UW in 1985, I remembered almost everything I learned in 25 years in college, including the six years in college before teaching. Every kind of paper, letters, lists, photographs, videotapes, audio tapes, artworks, and souvenirs—all these stayed with me the day that I walked away from the art building for good. Most important, I had a unique perspective of printmaking and its teaching, from the hands-on to the emerging world of virtual reality.

I saw two possibilities in higher education: Virtual and Virtuous. My gift of Nature is that I respect virtue and I would pursue this path; however, the virtual world is more real in academe, as things are not as they appear. The word virtual applies to optical illusions, such as the image you see in the mirror being a "virtual image."

The "real" image of education, in which I was a participant, was a real image because we—the students and I—shared an unspoken and vague partnership in learning that was more than the rhetorical speeches common in theoretical education.

This reality is a key to the development of fantasy printmaking trading card games in this book. The UW students taught me by demonstration during and after school that there are ten types of skills which would be useful to an artist's career. These ten are linked, not segmented, and not separated from each other in the ways a biology class is different from a speech class listed on a transcript.

Not segmented, but overlapping at their edges; or, taking three skill sets, they might form a fourth domain. This becomes complicated because intuition and guesswork play a big part in creative art—and it was the creativity of many of my former students that gave them a head start in the off-campus art world. They wanted to be professionals, and many learned things in subjects that were not thought to be important to an artist's career.

We took it upon ourselves to risk thinking outside the box. For example, we would drive several miles away from the campus to work in a TV studio on some days; or we'd walk to the far side of the campus and use the UW Hospital TV studios to make video art. We were, literally, outside the box of the old brick-and-mortar art building.

We would team up with students and faculty in music and dance performances, adding what we might to their exploration of new forms. The students in the performing arts planned to be professional artists after graduation, too. A few faculty besides me joined in.

Mine was a long, good college career, thanks to the students in my classes. Drawing on this experience I was able to create a map of our progress. This may would not have been necessary if I had not felt, deep inside, that I would probably not last the normal 40-year span of an art professor's tenure. It was probably the energy of the students' collective energy and intuition that drove me map out my own destiny and resign the job.

Ten skill areas came out of my period of reflecting on the previous nineteen years. How was I to proceed with the rest of my dual life as a teacher and artist? I distilled these ten areas from what the students and I had done together. Add to this what I had learned from my studies around the world, conferences that I had attended, workshops I conducted or too part in, and much reading, viewing and listening.

The ten skill areas are: (1) Cybernetics; (2) Electronic arts; (3) Time-based arts; (4) Social networking; (5) Printmaking; (6) Asset management; (7) Intellectual research; (78) Public speaking; (9) Video production; (10) Multimedia.

These ten skill areas are not sharply defined and distinctly separated, but I put them on "island domains" on a huge lake in my imaginary world. The cultures of the domains-of-expertise live up to their identity and serve the purpose of my life game. The islands are a focusing device.

For example, the island of printmaking is several moves away from the island of cybernetics, but in the realm of learning printmaking, one should remember the experience of learning that cybernetics is behind the design of the Internet. Navigation of the Internet is only one aspect of cybernetics, but it's important for the education of an artist this century.

The foreword to this book serves to tell part of the story as to why I think trading card games serve the student and practitioner of printmaking. In reading my attempt to steal the ideas of and re-design ten existing trading card games so that they fit my goal as a printmaking teacher, I hope to move the reader's learning experience forward.

A new printmaking experience is opening up, thanks to games with purpose.

Chapter 1: PrintWitch Coventry

PrintWitch Coventry is a fantasy printmaking TCG for 4-6 players, age 18+ where players role-play famous artists who endow the player with special powers. Players take on a second task of printer, curator, publisher or art dealer. There is only one art dealer and one publisher, but up to four muses and four nemeses, the PrintWitches, may be added. The art dealer owns the only Print Maker Faire. Everybody is out to get everybody in this game, and players must learn the ways of the printmaking world to win.

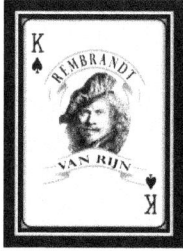 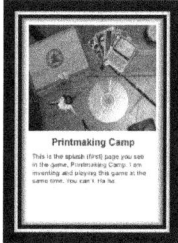

These are sample cards taken arbitrarily from the Emeralda City Library and used her as placeholders for actual cards.

We begin on ArtsPort Island, with an adaptation of an existing, real game named "Bang" which you can buy.

PrintWitch Coventry method of play which follows was written on July 13, 2013, on the Domain-of-Expertise, *ArtsPort*, which the domain of cyber world navigators. The reader is invited to edit and tune the text following until *PrintWitch Coventry* is a real, playable game—which will be hard work and not everyone can do it. For those who can, it will have its rewards.

Game Mechanic

At the start of the game, each player takes on the role of a famous artist who was not your typical commercial, industrial printmaker. Artists such as Rembrandt, Goya, Picasso or Rauschenberg. Each character endows the player with a special powers of during the game. The player role plays one of the famous artists who made contributions to printing that turned commercial printing on its head and made printing into a fine art.

Each player also gets a second printmaking task of printer, curator, publisher or art dealer. The duality is explained by the deep wisdom of the famous artist, having insights gained after years of working in the printmaking game. Thus the fine art printmaker knows a range of skills—even the secrets of publishing prints!

There is only <u>one art dealer</u> on the island, and only <u>one publisher</u>, but you can add in up to four Muses and four Nemeses. These are the PrintWitches and depends on the size of the group.

Everybody keeps his or her <u>job</u> private (face down) except for the <u>art dealer</u>—who owns the only Printmaking Roadshow on the island.

Your individual, specific goal (apart from just staying on the island) depends on your job.

1. The art dealer wants to bankrupt the publisher so she/he can take over the printing presses.
2. Each Muse wants to eliminate the Nemeses and help the artist grow in creative powers.
3. The nemeses (PrintWitches) want to ban both the art dealer and the publisher from the island altogether, as they work for the Omnium

Gatherum, creating a monopoly on all printmaking.
4. The Omnium Gatherum, with his vice-regents, the PrintWitch Coventry, wants to stifle all creative thinking on the island.

Gameplay centers on playing cards from your hand. (You ask how do you get the cards? You make them, silly, on your Kyber Press,[1] or you buy them as Preferred Stock shares in Emeralda).

To put another player at the table out of the game, you play a Spill-the-Bottle card (if you have one in your portfolio) a bottle of soda pop, wine, beer or milk that pours all over a Precious Print. The most powerful and destructive card of all is the Fire Card.

To stop the bottle from spilling its contents all over the Precious Print and ruining it beyond restoring, the other player might use the Laminate card (as a print in lamination is waterproof) or just play Grab-the-Bottle, Grab the Print, or Empty-the-Bottle so as to stop the bottle from spilling on and ruining the print.

To restore your health level you play a Take-A-Hike card. If you need a Take-A-Hike card, or any more cards, and you didn't get on in your starter deck, then you need to visit the ArtsPort Island Shop and buy a deck. Or, you can go online and download the printing plate that prints on your 3D printing plate printer. Of course, the decks are manufactured and may or may not have the card which you need.

No printmaking experience is complete without a Gates Prize upgrade—but beware of the Omnium Gatherum. He wants to smother all of us in CO^2!

---

[1] "Kyber press" was a name I made up to replace "Halfwood Press."

Web

In the online version, played on the Web, you can interact with the person closest to you on the PrintWorld Map of the Earth. This person is a Proximate, i.e., you found them using their Kyber Etching press at almost the same time as you were using your Kyber Press.

Back story: History of Emeralda Region

Emeralda Region was discovered by me in 1979. It happened one night in his basement studio. I had brought in a dumb terminal (which was the state of the art of modems at that time, used to communicate with the mainframe computer on campus, four miles away from Bill's home/studio) from the UW so that I could download from the mainframe and work with it in the convenience of his studio.

He hooked up the system, cradled his telephone hand piece on the device and retrieved his data. Then I was able to record the data on to a tape. From there his tape went into a tape player which was connected to his Apple II+, and ready to use as a text file.

Bill was looking for a certain pattern in the four columns of numbers on the screen and the printout. Each number in the four columns represented a point in three-dimensional space, an imaginary vacuum, a dark and unfathomable universe of the campus mainframe computer's database. Taken together, the X-Y-Z numbers would indicate a position in three-dimensional space, and the fourth number would represent a cone of vision of the "seeing eye". Taken together, it meant a point of view from which to examine an object described in another set of numbers.

Bill was working with these numbers to recreate a space-time event, like drawing frames in a cartoon, where each frame would present a kind of moving picture when the numbers were run in a connected sequence. This is an old idea, of course, dating back to medieval paintings, flip cards and motion pictures.

For me it was fascinating to try to read the numbers and use them to mentally construct the point-of-view and, next, try to estimate the effect of changing the cone-of-vision or any of the other four variables. This mental process had a mind-numbing effect, like the moment you doze off and wake up suddenly and realize you just experienced a mini-dream.

It was in this state of mind of his that the next thing happened that let me in on an amazing secret region I came to call, *Emeralda*, revealed in a most extraordinary way. It was like going through a fog bank and suddenly see the shoreline approaching, or descending through clouds and seeing a large, emerald-green lake below. Satisfied with the data, I made the edits I wanted to print out the next day and, connecting with the computer lab again via the dumb terminal, uploaded the data to the distant campus. But there was more to come, an even stranger experience.

Now I wanted to write about it, and I opened the text program on the Apple, called *Apple Writer*, and started typing. The screen of this computer (some people may remember) was black—and the characters and numbers appeared in an acidic, bright, fluorescent lime green. It was after I had typed a few letters that the phenomenal thing happened that changed my life.

Maybe it was because by now it was getting late, and his wife called down to me that the girls wanted me to come up and say goodnight. I answered, Yes I would—in a minute; and I turned back to the screen to resume what I was doing when she had called. No sooner than I had typed a single word that the words began to type themselves! Not in the sense of an automatic, spell-checker or word-completion program, but more like his fingers were only <u>uncovering words that already were on the screen</u>, but covered in the black.

He was, in other words, <u>erasing the black that hid the words,</u> and the words were not his. They couldn't be his, because I had never thought or heard of such a place as the region which, after a few moments, was described on the screen. It was the beginning of a history of the region going back billions of years, with an incident occurring three hundred centuries before Bill's time, or 30,000 BCE.

That moment changed Bill's life; whereas I had been living an ordinary, orderly life as a college art professor before I started working with computers in line with his field of printmaking, now I was given the belief that Emeralda really existed and that I was chosen to know about it. I alone would be able to delve deeply into the region and learn the meaning of life taken in perspective of a 30,000 year view and—this is the scary part—events that I would experience for the remainder of his life.

I was only 39 years old when this happened. I and his wife had been married for fifteen years and they had two daughters, ten and seven years old. They lived in a grand, hip-roof craftsman house on the side of Queen

Anne Hill—a nice urban neighborhood in Seattle. I had been working at the university since 1966—hired at the early age of 26. His experiments with video art and, now, computers, had some people guessing why a printmaker was dabbling in technologies that, to them, are extraneous to fine art.

Now my life took a new direction toward game design. With the games I want to play, I want to invite everyone to share in the quest for a way to get into, and out of, the imaginary world of Emeralda Region.

Origin of Printwitch Coventry

The model for "PrintWitch Coventry" is "Bang," a collectible card game described in "Trading Card Games for Dummies," Page 300. This article first appeared as a 'Zine essay, ap1300713, an entry in ArtsPort's TCG games.

Chapter 2: Richter five

Richter five is a Fantasy Printmaking Trading Card Game for 2 to 10 players. Played with 108 special numbered cards and each one includes one or more items that are found in printmaking studios and printmaking trivia to keep things interesting and make the game educational, plus earthquake trivia. The year is 1776 and there's likely to be an onslaught of aftershocks after the earthquake that caused the Great Wave shown in Hokusai's print. Another quake is coming and if it catches you inside a cave you're dead! You must play your cards right to get out before the Big One hits. Score the fewest points and win the game.

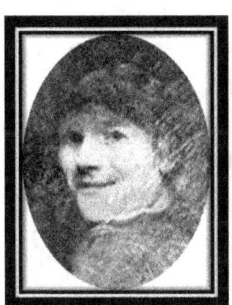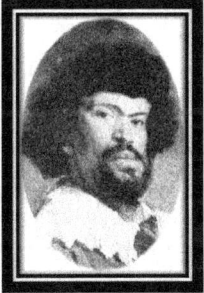

These are sample cards taken arbitrarily from the Emeralda City Library and used her as placeholders for actual cards.

For E'Studios Island, adapting a real game named "6 Nimmi (Six Takes)" which you can buy.

Bill Ritchie, Emeralda designer, reassembled the German game, *6 Nimmi* (meaning 'six takes') for the printmaking world market by making variations on the rules and wrapping the whole thing up in an earthquake theme.

The earthquake idea originated in the Ballad of Vladimir, which is found in the back of the 2013 edition of *Halfwood Press: The Story*, about the fate of the evil First Mate. *Richter 5* is the medium-strength quake that it took to bury the bad guy in the story. Another source is the screenplay, *Swipe.*

Richter Five consists of a deck containing 108 numbered cards. In addition to the number on the card, each one includes one or more items that are found in printmaking studios, plus printmaking trivia to keep things interesting and make the game mildly educational. Cards also have earthquake trivia, such as the historic earthquakes of the past and potential earthquake disasters, earthquake science, etc.

There is no connection between earthquakes and printmaking, by the way. We just thought it necessary to add it in because printmaking is our meta-game here at E'Studios in the imaginary world of Emeralda Region.

The promotional text for Richter Five reads:

"It's 1776 and there's likely to be an onslaught of aftershocks after the earthquake in the Pacific Ocean that caused the Great Wave. Another quake is about to happen on your island! If it catches you inside the cave with the First Mate, you're dead! Play your cards with logic, play your cards with strategy, or play your cards with blind luck; <u>but don't get caught in the cave</u>: get out before the Big One hits! Richter Five will bring the whole cliff sliding down and bury you! Avert disaster and you won't pick up unwanted cards or points. Score the fewest points and win the game."

Play starts by dealing a hand of ten cards to each player. The Dealer then turns up four more cards in the center of the table, starting four rows. These rows are central to the game—they will get longer until they reach the sixth card you place after the fifth card because of the numbering system.

Each turn happens simultaneously, which means all the plays take a turn at the same time. Players take one card from their hand and lay it face down in front of them. When all players have a card ready, face down in front of them, they all flip the cards over at the same moment. This makes the game begin.

The player with the lowest numbered card goes first, with the rest of the players going in ascending numeric order according to their up-facing card number. Looking at the four 'ROW' cards on the table, each player in turn tries to place his card next to the last card in a row that is the <u>closest number lower</u> than his card.

For example, if the four rows start with 11, 17, 21, and 40, then a 20 card would go next to the 17 because that's the lowest number near the player's card, 20. Having put his card by the 17, now 20 is the end card in that row. The other rows are 11, 21 and 40, and now the 20 is at the end of the row with 17 next to it.

The player with the lowest number of points wins at the end of the game, so when the next, following conditions are reached, you need to do some math by adding the total of the numbers on the cards, which total gives you your points. You want the lowest number of points, comparable to the lowest number on the Richter Scale, the earthquakes of the lowest order and least damaging.

(It helps to have read the story about Vladimir Chichinoff and the evil First Mate in the *Ballad of*

Vladimir, also the screenplay, *Swipe,* and it is helpful to want to learn about printmaking.)

We left off with the 20th card. Now several situations could happen.

1. If you played next to a number that's lower than your card and your card is NOT the sixth card one in that row, your part of the turn ends uneventfully. This is good for you.

2. If you played next to a number that's lower than your card, but the row already had five other cards, the you take the five cards, put them in your Scoring Pile (your cave) and place what would have been the sixth card, your card, in the starting position of the row you collected. It means you scored points, which you don't want to do because it is a low number of points that gets you out of the cave when the Big One hits.

3. If your card is lower than the final number in each and every row, then, as always, you must take one of those rows; you get to choose which one. You should pick the one with the fewest printmaking tools and other items on its card face and put this set in your scoring pile. Then put your low-number card in the row to begin a new row.

After ten rounds of play, count the number of printmaking items in your score pile, write the number down on your score sheet, and then a new round begins with a new deal of the cards, i.e., each player is dealt ten cards again. Your score sheet is before you, awaiting the results.

When someone among the players hits 5.0 on the Richter scale, it means they were safely far away from the cave when the intensity of the earthquake reached that critical level. This player, who has the lowest point total, wins the game.

Buy it now

If the shop exists by now, you may visit the E'Studios Island Shop and buy a deck for this game. Or, you can go online and download the printing plate that prints on your 3D plate printer. Of course, the decks are manufactured and may or may not have the card you need.

Gates Prize Upgrade

No printmaking experience is complete without a Gates Prize upgrade—but beware of the Omnium Gatherum. He wants to smother all of us in CO^2. The motive of all Emeralda Games is to destroy the shade, Ominium Gatherum, and all that this shade stands for.

In the online version, played on the Web, it may be possible that you can interact with the person closest to you on the PrintWorld Map of the Earth. This person is a Proximate, i.e., you found them using their Kyber Etching press at almost the same time as you were using your Kyber Press.

Origin of the gameplay for "Richter Five"

Based on "Category 5: Beware the Sixth Card in a Row," a trading card game described in "Trading Card Games for Dummies," Page 301.

Back story: History of Emeralda Region

What I discovered in Emeralda Region, after many years of exploring the area, was that there are ten islands of notable size and cultural development. The culture of the residents varies, although all the communities were essentially "print-centric." That is, they were of the unanimous opinion that all technologies today are descended from the simplest kinds of printing—hand prints either stenciled or printed by relief methods on walls of caves.

While the simplest print by a human being is probably the footprint, if you think about it the handprint is considered the true ancestor of printmaking because the handprint is <u>intentional</u>. The handprints on the walls of caves or found on other protected stone surfaces were put there on purpose, whereas footprints are accidental—merely the incidental marks left by walking on mud, for example.

The routine of an Emeralda resident is a daily visit to one of the ten islands in the order in which they are named, alphabetically. The first day is spent in ArtsPort; the second day (the day of this writing in this series of Trading Card Game design exercises) is at E'Studios.

E'Studios is an abbreviation of "Electronic Studios and Art Galleries." The culture here, although it is print-centric, is one of electronic arts of all kinds. Video art, computer art and multimedia arts, certainly, but on the traditional side the use of electricity in galvanic etching is another way the cultural practices are carried on here.

The choice of the game as a starting point for Richter Five was a choice set arbitrarily in the book, Trading Card Games for Dummies, Part V, where the author offered up ten easy games to help the novice get into the swing of card games of the kind that underlie many TCGs.

The promotional copy, above, was adapted from the Website for Category 5, a game company called Pando. As with PrintWitch, the exercise prior to this one, a back story is in order to tie the earthquake theme to Richter Five. The goal is to make an Emeralda Game, and the back story given thus far explains how I discovered Emeralda.

There's plenty of time to contemplate the origins of printmaking in Emeralda, as printmaking is the core culture here. It was inevitable that the printing press would be a subject of study, and this brings us to the back story for Richter Five.

As the copy above said, something happened in 1776 that was of momentous importance. The scene was a sheltered cove in a region very much like Emeralda Region except that it was open to the Pacific Ocean. (Emeralda Region landlocked, its main feature is a great lake dotted with islands around its perimeter).

There was, at the time, a ship anchored in the cove. It was a three-mast frigate named the *Emeralda*. Yes, the Emeralda Region shares the name, but it is only a coincidence. Among the ships passengers and crew were a Russian boy about fourteen years old, an old navigator, and another Russian who had been rescued after his ship was wrecked in a storm. He had been first mate of that craft and was the only survivor.

Coincidentally, the teenage boy, too, had been rescued too, but not from the storm. He had been cast off from that same, other ship a month before the storm. He was left to die. As fate would have it, it had been the First Mate—now rescued by the Emeralda crew—who had engineered the boy's vanquish. Strange it is that the two were the only survivors; both the victim and his tormentor were stuck together again, this time on a foreign, European ship.

It gets worse. One night a rogue wave swept into the channel from the Pacific Ocean—result of a Richter 7 quake far out in the ocean. The narrowing channel by which the wave found its way into the islands caused it to rise to a great height and with such force that it lifted the frigate and smashed it against the rock cliffs above the cove—like a giant's great, watery hand smashing an egg.

Everyone died except the boy and the first mate. The funny thing is that the First Mate had purposely got the boy left ashore the previous day—which is why the boy's life was saved. Abandoned, he found shelter for the night in a shallow cave above the rocky walls of the cove. The morning after the disaster hit, he looked out on the destruction left by the wave and the ship was gone.

When he made his way down to the wrack and ruin, he found many of dead bodies of the crew amid what was left of the ship. He found the old navigator, his mentor. He was dead. The navigator's pet monkey was beside him, having a screaming fit. And—not far away—lying in a tangle of ships' rope and splintered timbers, fate revealed a terrible blow because there was the First Mate and he was alive.

Badly bruised and with a leg broken, yet he was alive. The boy was the kind of person who could not leave him to die despite of the murderous tricks the man had played on him. He had tried to kill him on more than one occasion. Nevertheless, the boy untangled the unconscious man, put a splint on his leg and dragged him to his little sheltering cave.

He returned to the wreckage to salvage what he could. He found one of the printing presses, its chest still intact and the press wrapped in oilskin, sealed against the water—just as it had been when it left the north coast of Spain over a year ago. This, as well as some ships biscuits and a few tools, the boy carried back to the cave.

When the First Mate gained consciousness, he ranted and cursed at the boy—almost insane with pain and angry with his situation as he was dependent on the boy. As for the boy, he had a kind of hope in that caring for the First Mate gave him purpose in life; and also it pleased him he was such a thorn in the invalid's side.

This, then, is the back story for Richter Five, and gives you an idea as to what the images on the cards mean. The game players know that after a quake of Richter 7, there will be aftershocks. No one can predict whether they will be minor tremors or another major earthquake.

The game is played with the threat of another earthquake—and this time not a thousand miles out to sea but close by—right in the area of the island. A quake of Richter Five will certainly bring down the ceiling over the cave because it is gravelly clay and sandstone and would not stand the strain of an earthquake of that magnitude.

How will you fare when Richter Five hits? When the cards are added up, and 5.0 is attained, the ceiling of the cave will come tumbling down and bury everything—and every one—inside. It depends on whether the total is an even or an odd number.

An even number means the player is outside. The player is in the role of the boy, of course, the good guy. This makes it easy to remember, because he "gets even" with the bad guy in a way.

However, if the total is the number is odd, then the boy is trapped inside with the bad guy and the boy—which is the role you play—perishes. You die and you are out of the game.

Richter Five is the second of the games to be written down in a more-or-less cogent way. The method of play, above, was written on July 14, 2013, on the Domain-of-Expertise called "E'Studios," which is for electronic art and art galleries.

You are invited to edit, tune and hack the text above until it is a better, real, workable game. It will be hard work, but promises to be rewarding.

Chapter 3: Beryl Galore

A Fantasy Printmaking Trading Card Game, for 3 to 5 players, is a fascinating card game based on four colors: green, red, yellow and blue—the RGB colors in electronic media yielding millions of colors, and four colors—cyan, yellow, magenta and black—also known as CYMK that we get colors in printed media. The game is based on the myth, Women Who Fell to Earth, in which, about three-hundred centuries ago, a sextuplet of aliens came to Earth from the planet Fleura. Five-to-one, they came with good intentions. Since Earth's scientists have forecast the end of Earth's human life sustainability by the year 2022, time is running out! When you play Beryl Galore, you seek solutions to the world's Union of Concerned Scientists' Five Principles to save Earth's human life sustainability with the help of printmaking art.

 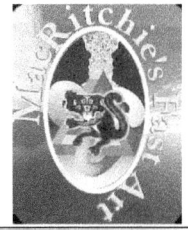

These are sample cards taken arbitrarily from the Emeralda City Library and used her as placeholders for actual cards.

The promotional text for Beryl Galore reads:

"Three-hundred centuries ago four aliens—four women and two men—came to Earth from the planet Fleura. Why they chose Earth we do not know, or for what purpose. We only know that Earth's scientists are forecasting the end of this planet's human life sustainability by the year 2022. Time is running out!

When you play Beryl Galore, you might find solutions to the scientists' stated Five Principle Ways to save Earth's human life sustainability through art."

Based on the myth, *Women Who Fell to Earth*, *Beryl Galore* is a fascinating card game based on four colors: green, red, yellow and blue. You might know about the color on printing press techniques that gives us the millions of colors based on four colors—cyan, yellow, magenta and black—also known as CYMK. Or, in video, red, green and blue—RGB.

The four color idea for a color-based card game emerged from the myth, where four women (and two brothers) came to Earth 30,000 years ago in a spacecraft from Fleura. Each of the sisters is characterized by a color. You need to know that, on Fleura, the mineral beryl (beryllium aluminum cyclosilicate) is as common to Fleurians as is basalt is here. In other words, it makes up about 90% of the planet's stone components.

Without going into too much detail, there is beryl everywhere on Fleura—on the shores of the oceans, on rock outcroppings, there are entire mountains of the mineral. Beryl, here on Earth, is also known as a precious stone that is found in six colors: (1) green, (2) blue, (3) yellow, (4) pink, (5) red and (6) clear. As gems they are called (1) emerald, (2) aquamarine, (3) yellow beryl, (4) morganite, (5) red beryl and (6) goshenite.

Beryl Galore consists of a deck containing 108 numbered and colored cards. In addition to the number and dominant color on the card, each one includes one or more items that are found in printmaking studios, plus multimedia trivia to keep things interesting and make the game mildly educational.

Cards also have trivia from the back story myth, such as the history of the Fleurians' coming to Earth, the mystery of why the Fleurians came, and scientific evidence pointing to environmental disasters, ecology, and Earth's future human life sustainability.

There is a connection between the myth and fast printmaking, by the way and it's necessary to add it in because fast art printmaking is our meta-game here at MacRitchie's Fast Art in Emeralda Region.

Play starts by starting one row of cards in the center of the table for each player. The first player flips the top card from the color deck and places that card into one of the rows. From that point on, each player gets a very simple choice: Draw a card and add it to a row, or take all the cards in a row and add them to their score pile of cards.

If the player adds a card to a row, nothing else happens in the turn, and the next player goes into action. Because each row holds a maximum of three cards, individual rows fill up pretty quickly. You must pay close attention to the colors each player has in his or her pile before tossing a card into a row. Otherwise, you might create a row with only the colors that another player wants for his or her collection!

After taking a row, the player adds the cards from that row into the color piles in front of her, and then sits out the rest of the turn. After all the rows get taken, players create new rows and the process begins anew. Play continues until someone pulls the end-of-round marker from the top of the draw deck, at which point everybody takes one of the current rows, and the game is over.

You never know what card might come off the deck next, so luck plays a solid part in this game. But Beryl Galore still features plenty of strategic potential. You need lots of cards to score the biggest points, however, strategically you need to make an if-then decision:

A: Should you grab a row that contains fewer than the three cards if it has only the right color s for your collection? Or . . .

B: Should you go for the big rows that pour scads of cards into your stacks in hopes of earning the biggest bonuses at the end of the game without racking up too many minuses? The person with the most points wins the game.

Which strategy is best? Only time will tell—you have to play to know.

To play the game, it helps to know the story, *Women Who Fell to Earth* and the novel, *Hunt for the Emeralda Treasure*. It is helpful to want to learn about printmaking, too. Most of all, it is mandatory to know the 1992 publication, *Earth's Scientists Warning to Humanity*, by the *Union of Concerned Scientists*. This little pamphlet started Bill on his journey to Emeralda Region and is always watching his back.

Visit the MacRitchie's Fast Art Island Shop and buy a deck for this game. Or, you can go online and download the printing plate that prints on your 3D plate printer. Of course, the decks are manufactured and may or may not have the card you need.

Gates Prize Upgrade

No printmaking experience is complete without a Gates Prize upgrade—but beware of the Omnium

Gatherum. He wants to smother all of us in CO^2. The motive of all Emeralda Games is to destroy the Ominium Gatherum and all that this shade stands for.

In the online version, played on the Web, it may be possible that you can interact with the person closest to you on the PrintWorld Map of the Earth. This person is a Proximate, i.e., you found them using their Kyber Etching press at almost the same time as you were using your Kyber Press.

Origin of "Beryl Galore"

Based on "Coloretto: Collecting Colors and Thinking Fast," a trading card game for 3 to 5 players, costing about $12 and described in "Trading Card Games for Dummies," Page 302. Interestingly, another small, 10 card, cut-them-yourself expansion for Coloretto came out from Michael Schacht's own Spiele Aus Timbuktu, containing 2 variations for the game (one with 8 new extra cards and one with 2 new line cards). It was published in a limited edition of 1999 units. These were also re-published in 2012 in a professionally produced promo that was distributed through BoardGameGeek. This version comes with 6 extra cards, plus two new score cards on the backs of the rule cards.

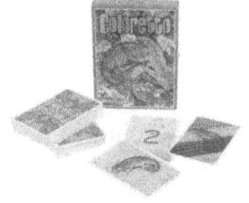
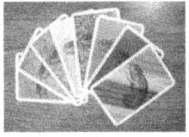

Back story: History of Emeralda Region and MacRitchie's Island's place in it

In the cyberspace of his imaginary place, Emeralda Region, I explored for ten years starting in 1992. I was searching for the Holy Grail of learning media arts—where they came from and where the media arts were leading.

The routine of an Emeralda resident like me is a daily visit to one of the ten islands in the order in which the islands are named, alphabetically. The first day is spent in ArtsPort; the second day, E'Studios and the third day—today—is spent at MacRitchie's Fast Free Fine Art, or, simply, "MacRitchie's." On this island the culture centers on ways to make fine art with great speed and efficiency.

The name was inspired by Macdonald's, trend-setter in the fast food industry. I changed the name to fit his own Scottish heritage and then I did some Imagineering on the subject of ways computer imaging would be fit for fine art in the future.

Of each of the ten islands in Emeralda Region, the culture differs from one compared to the next. However, all the communities are essentially "print-centric," which means that the cultural teaching, research and practices are based on the plain truth that all technologies today are descended from the simplest kind of printing.

Printmaking is the root of all modern technologies. The simplest "printing" by a human being is the footprint. The handprint, however, is the real ancestor of printmaking because the handprint is intentional. The handprints on the walls of caves or found on other protected stone surfaces were put there on purpose, while footprints are merely incidental.

Footprints are useful as indicators of direction and, we assume, purpose. The famous tracks discovered sometimes suggest, for example, that a group was walking along and one stopped and turned aside. Why did they pause? Perhaps it was so they could smell the roses that grew along the path. We speculate about people by studying incidental foot prints, but hand prints are intentional and gave rise to the idea of making templates to mechanically reproduce the image of themselves. That's why printmaking is different from drawing, painting, and sculpture: printmaking is mechanical.

The choice of the game, Coloretto, as a starting point for Beryl Galore was a choice set arbitrarily in the book, *Trading Card Games for Dummies*, Part V, where the author offered up ten easy games to help the novice get into the swing of card games of the kind that underlie many TCGs. This fits nicely with the ten-island campaign to discover ATC/TCG of Emeralda.

The promotional copy, above, was drawn from my myth of the four women and two men—a sextuplet, actually—as his game back story. As with PrintWitch, and Richter Five, a back story is in order to tie the color theme to Emeralda games.

There's plenty of time to contemplate the origins of printmaking in Emeralda, as printmaking is the core culture here. It was inevitable that the printing press would be a subject of study, and this brings us to the back story for Beryl Galore.

Something happened 30,000 years ago that was of momentous importance. One of the alien's craft splashed down in the sea, and she—her name was Media—would have drowned if she had not been rescued by a dolphin.

In a cave accessible only by a water passage in southern France area (known as the Cosquer region), this Fleurian, Media, encountered a group of women in a cavern. They had a secret passageway from the camp above and it was in this cavern that they practiced their arts—painting, drawing and sculpting. Also singing, because the cavern had wonderful acoustics.

The specter of paintings illuminated by torches, the chanting and all made for an experience like a concert. Imagine their surprise when Media burst upon them from a pool—the outlet of the underwater passage she came through to reach the cavern.

My story has twists and turns, too lengthy for the purposes of describing the back story for Beryl Galore. One thing that must be known is that before Media came on the scene, all art was painting, drawing and sculpture. She introduced printing—the basis of which is the template—in an accidental way and, by so doing, unleashed the mechanistic side, the media arts as we know the arts of print, video and computer graphics that we take for granted today.

Conclusion to Chapter 3

Beryl galore is the third of the games suggested on July 15, 2013, on the Domain-of-Expertise called "MacRitchie's Fast, Free Fine Art," which is for making fine art with great speed and intention.

You are invited to edit, tune and hack the text above until it is a better, real, workable game. It will be hard work, but it is fun and rewarding, this is a promise.

Chapter 4: Blue Crown

A Fantasy Printmaking Trading Card Game for 1 to 8 players. Blue Crown consists of a deck containing 54 numbered and colored cards, each printed with selected Rembrandt self-portraits and on five colors: red, green, blue, yellow and black. You score points by matching the four parts of the cards (they are sliced up) to make a whole card. In addition to the number and dominant color on the card, each one includes one or more items that are found in Rembrandt's etching studios, plus multimedia trivia to keep things interesting and make the game educational. Cards also have trivia from the novel, "Rembrandt's Ghost in the New Machine," incidents encountered by the time traveler in 1660, facts about Rembrandt's life and work, and fictional characters. See if you can assemble the entire card collection.

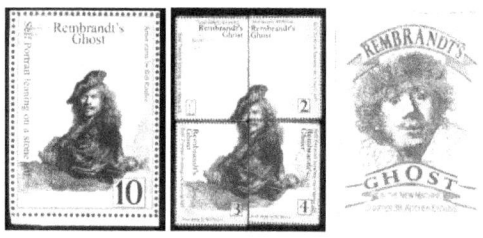

These are images of Rembrandt's Ghost cards and tiles under development and used here as placeholders for actual cards and tiles. Left: full card; Middle: tiled card; Right, first Playing card back

The promotional text for Blue Crown reads:

"Three-hundred fifty years ago a famous playing card producer named Jacques van Leest wanted the famous painter, Rembrandt, to print etchings as playing cards but the artist was down on his luck, with no press until, like magic, a time traveler arrived with a miniature press suited to card-printing. The painter secretly printed artist cards until the time traveler, and his press, disappeared. See if you can assemble the entire card collection before Rembrandt's time is up!"

Based on the novel, *Rembrandt's Ghost in the New Machine*, the collectible trading card game, *Blue Crown*, is a fascinating card game based on five colors: red, green, blue, yellow and black. You might know about the color on printing press techniques that gives us the millions of colors based on either four colors—cyan, yellow, magenta and black (also known as CYMK) or red, green and blue—RGB—in video.

The five color idea for this color-based card game emerged from the novel, "Rembrandt's Ghost in the New Machine," when a 21st Century printmaker time-travels back to 1660. He has a miniature etching press with me which he uses to print Artist Trading Cards. By coincidence, he encounters Rembrandt in his last years and at the bottom of his career. The famous painter pins his hopes on a come-back on—of all things—playing cards. When Rembrandt sees the mini press, his hopes soar because the press is all he needs to start producing the worlds' first Artist Trading Cards.

Something about Artist Trading Cards plus Rembrandt's etchings and a tiny etching press is what inspired me to design this game, "Blue Crown." The game takes a very simple premise—connecting chains of color together—and builds a very visual and highly re-playable game out of it.

Blue Crown consists of a deck containing 54 numbered and colored cards, each printed with images of Rembrandt self-portraits. You score points by connecting the four parts of the cards (they are sliced up) to make a whole card. In addition to the number and dominant color on the card, each one includes one or more items that are found in Rembrandt's etching studios, plus multimedia trivia to keep things interesting and make the game mildly educational.

Cards also have trivia from the back story novel, such as the incidents encountered by the time traveler, historic facts about Rembrandt's life and work, and fictional characters roles in the novel.

A footnote to this game is that here is a connection between the novel, "Rembrandt's Ghost . . ." and hospitality, because O'Studios—the island in Emeralda Region—is all about "Open Studios and Hospitality" of the same kind that the time traveler in the book enjoys in 1660 Amsterdam. Hospitality and entertainment is the meta-game on the island-of-domain-of-expertise, O'Studios, in Emeralda Region.

Play starts by shuffling the corner pieces—tiles that make up complete cards—and stack them face (colored) side down. Then, the starting player flips over two random tiles and places them side-by side in the center of the table so the outer edges match with outer edges—if they can be matched. If not, they are set corner-to-corner.

Next this player flips a third tile and starts playing the game. You get a point for each color on your tile with the same color on the other tile. If the three tiles at the beginning of the game . . . .

Time is running out, as the time traveler will be recalled to the 21st Century when he or she turns over the last of the four quadrants that make the copper plate.

Does this make sense? "If the player adds a card to a row, nothing else happens in the turn, and the next player goes into action."

Does this make sense? "Because each row holds a maximum of three cards, individual rows fill up pretty quickly."

Does this make sense? "You must pay close attention to the colors each player has in his or her pile before tossing a card into a row.

Does this make sense? "Otherwise, you might create a row with only the colors that another player wants for his or her collection!

Does this make sense? "After taking a row, the player adds the cards from that row into the color piles in front of her, and then sits out the rest of the turn.

Does this make sense? "After all the rows get taken, players create new rows and the process begins anew.

Does this make sense? "Play continues until someone pulls the end-of-round marker from the top of the draw deck, at which point everybody takes one of the current rows, and the game is over.

Does this make sense? "You never know what quadrant might come off the deck next, so luck plays a solid part in this game. But Blue Crown still features plenty of strategic potential. You need lots of tiles to score the biggest points, however, strategically you need to make an if-then decision:

…

Does this make sense? "Which strategy is best? Only time will tell—you have to play to know.

To play the game, it's necessary to know the story, *Rembrandt's Ghost in the New Machine*. It is helpful to want to learn about printmaking, too. Most of all, it is mandatory to know the 1992 publication, *Earth's Scientists Warning to Humanity*, by the *Union of Concerned Scientists*. This little pamphlet started me on my journey to Emeralda Region and is always watching my back.

Visit the O'Studios' Island Shop and buy a deck for this game. Or, you can go online and download the printing plate that prints on your 3D plate printer. Of course, the decks are manufactured and may or may not have the card you need.

Gates Prize Upgrade

No printmaking experience is complete without a Gates Prize upgrade—but beware of the Omnium Gatherum. He wants to smother all of us in CO^2. The motive of all Emeralda Games is to destroy the Ominium Gatherum and all that this shade stands for.

In the online version, played on the Web, it may be possible that you can interact with the person closest to you on the PrintWorld Map of the Earth. This person is a Proximate, i.e., you found them using their Kyber Etching press at almost the same time as you were using your Kyber Press.

Origin of "Blue Crown"

"Blue Crown" is based on "Continuo: Great for Younger Kids and Non-Gaming Friends," a trading card game for 1 to 8 players, costing about $12 and described in "Trading Card Games for Dummies," Page 303.

Further back in time than this game, we find ourselves in the 17th Century and looking into the life of a playing-card maker named Jacques van Leest. His story is told briefly in an entry at the Speelkaartenmuseum (playing card museum) in The Netherlands.

Jacques van Leest was a playing-card maker, mapmaker, and paper seller. His address is given as: *Amsterdam, on the water, "in the blue crown"*. He lived from 1612 to 1665. Leest's cards had a map images and also, "The Cygnet", "Ship", "Carpenter" and "Three Hammers". He owned a number of houses and, in 1660, the painter Rembrandt van Rijn rented a house from him. Rembrandt put his signature to the deed with Van Leest. True story.

Back story: Emeralda Region and O'Studios' Island

Starting in 1992 and continuing for ten years, I explored his imaginary place in his cyberspace. I named it, Emeralda Region. I was searching for the Holy Grail of experiencing the ever-changing world of teaching, researching and practicing the vast domain of the media arts—where these arts originated and where the path was leading.

The routine of an Emeralda resident like me daily visiting one of the ten islands in the order in which the islands are named, alphabetically. The first day is spent in ArtsPort; the second day, E'Studios and so on. The fourth day—today—is spent on Open Studios and Hospitality, or, simply, "O'Studios." On this island the culture is about fun, food and friendly artists and, sometimes, on the ways to make great fine art through collaboration and teamwork.

The name was inspired by the occasional "Open Studio" you see offered by individual artists or art communities. Art galleries and museums sometime coordinate an "Art Walk" and, in Seattle, the First Thursdays has been a success for years. I did some thinking on the subject of ways these social events figure for fine art in teaching research, practice and service—his idea of the perfect studio.

Of each of the ten islands in Emeralda Region, the culture differs from one compared to the next. However, all the communities are essentially "print-centric," which means that the cultural teaching, research and practices are based on the plain truth that all technologies today are descended from the simplest kind of printing.

Printmaking is the root of all modern technologies and the history of technology is sprinkled with chance occurrences and people meeting to work on shared ideas.

The choice of the game, Continuo Card Game as a starting point for Blue Crown was a choice I made arbitrarily in the book, *Trading Card Games for Dummies*, Part V, where the author offered up a series of ten easy games to help me get into the swing of card games of the kind that are the basis of some TCGs. The number fits nicely with the ten-island campaign to discover ATC/TCG of Emeralda.

The promotional copy, above, was drawn from my novel, *Rembrandt's Ghost in the New Machine* as one of his games' back stories. As with PrintWitch, Richter

Five, and Beryl Galore, a back story helps tie the printmaking theme to Emeralda Trading Card Games.

The back story for Blue Crown is tied to a real printing press known as the Mini Halfwood Press. Just as the story is told, the press is suitable for printing playing-card sized etchings and other kinds of printing plates. This includes the newest kind, the 3-D printed collagraphs.

Something happened in Rembrandt's time because a few artists thought outside the box and extended the printing techniques to fit their artistic bent. Instead of staying with the normal way of the printing business, where mass production was the only goal, they worked on their plates with freedom, giving printmaking the same creative treatment that made their paintings memorable for all time.

My story about my imaginary visit to Rembrandt (in a thinly-disguised autobiographical sketch) has twists and turns, too much for the purposes of describing the back story for Blue Crown.

Conclusion to Chapter 4

Blue Crown is the fourth of the games outlined in a sketchy way. The method of play, above, was written on July 16, 2013, on the Domain-of-Expertise called "Open Studios and Hospitality," which is for artists to share their studio experience with society and participate in social networking and demonstrations to shed light on the creative process. The reader is invited to edit, tune and hack the text above until it is a better, real, workable game. It will be hard work, but it is fun and rewarding, this is a promise.

Chapter 5: Tets

A Fantasy Printmaking Trading Card Game for 4 to 8 players (singles or doubles only) based on the novels, *Women Who Fell to Earth* and *Hunt for the Emeralda Treasure*, is a collectible trading card game in which the starting player tosses tetrahedron dice called *Tets* in the center of the table, totals the unseen numbers, and starts playing the game. Total points are written score cards. Players then may draw that number of cards from the deck of Artist Trading Cards, which are face down. *Tets*, is based on four colors: red, green, blue, and yellow—the colors used in media arts. The prize at the end of the game is to open the first of the Tets. Inside is a numbered printing plate, and the higher the number, the bigger the win.

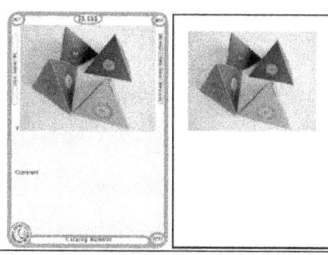

These two cards are placeholders. They show what the Tets look like, the special "dice" for Tets.

The descriptive text for Tets reads:

"Tets is a strategy game for 2 to 4 players, ages 8 years and up. First player to collect 3 prizes and keep them until the beginning of their next turn wins. The box includes 4 tetrahedron dice, 10 prizes, a dice cup and rules of play. The optional timer may be purchased separately"

Based on my novels, *Women Who Fell to Earth* and *Hunt for the Emeralda Treasure*, the collectible trading card game, *Tets*, is a fascinating dice and card game based on four colors: red, green, blue, and yellow. You might know about the color on printing press techniques that gives us the millions of colors based on either four colors—cyan (blue), yellow, magenta (red) and black (also known as CYMK). This is a game about printing, however, so black gets green as a substitute color, borrowed from the four types of beryl (from *Women Who . . .*).

The four color idea for this color-based game emerged from the novels, when four women—sisters in a sextuplet—from "The Flower Planet," *Fleura*, come to Earth, each in her own module from the mother ship. Each of the alien women carries a souvenir stone from her planet—the forms of beryl we know as the precious gems, emerald, morganite, aquamarine and yellow beryl. Something about the stones describes the personality of each sister. These are their properties, or attributes.

Tets consists of a deck containing 54 numbered and colored cards, each printed with images from the two novels. You score points by "tossing the *Tets*" and counting the total of the sides that you cannot see. For example if you can see a 1, 3, and 4 on the sides of the tetrahedron, then the unseen side has to be 2.

The cards also have trivia from the back story novel, such as the incidents encountered by the sisters and related to each other as they search for their brothers. These women are immortals. In the past 300 centuries they have encountered human beings of note, and they brag about the clever ways they manipulated these humans and which manipulations led to these peoples' greatness.

There is a connection between the novels and printmaking, by the way and it's necessary to add it in because Perfect Press—the island in emerald Region where this game originated—is all about printmaking and the kind of trivia, technique and historic facts that make up the culture on this island in Emeralda Region.

The starting player tosses the *Tets* in the center of the table. Next this player totals the unseen numbers and starts playing the game. You get the total as points, write them on your score card and then you may draw that number of cards from the deck of Artist Trading Cards, which are face down.

Time plays in *Tets*, as by the year 2022 it will be all over with for humans. Or, if successful, then scientists realize the benefits of working with artistic game designers. The prize at the end of the game is that you get to open the first of the Tets. Inside is a numbered printing plate, and the higher the number, the bigger the win.

Time may play another part in *Tets* because there is a tetrahedron-shaped timer (about $30) called the *DGT Pyramid* available in game stores. It is for Chess, poker, and other games where there are rules about response-time.

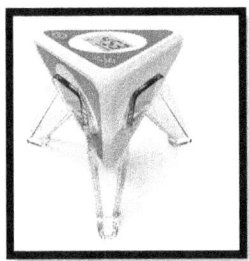

It is very cool and looks like the *Tets*, even has four colors. The promotional copy is:

> "The DGT Pyramid is a colorful multi-player game timer with four separate clocks - one on each side. It is suitable for any table top game or board game with up to four players. Whether it is a competitive game at the club or a friendly game at home, the DGT Pyramid adds fun, fairness and excitement. A motion sensor ensures that only the clock facing upwards is running. Simply turn the DGT Pyramid in its base and the next player's clock will automatically start to run. Place the Pyramid on the table outside its base to pause all clocks and interrupt the game for example when disputing a word in a game of Scrabble.
> The DGT Pyramid has five different timing options:
> -Game timer option: each player has the same amount of time to complete the whole game; each time a player's clock is faced upwards his clock will continue counting down.
> -Move timer option: each player has the same amount of time to complete each turn or move; at the start of each turn each player again receives the same amount of time in which to complete the move.
> -Move timer + save option: as in the move timer option each player receives the same amount of time at the start of each turn, but in addition with the move timer save option all time a player has not used on its

previous moves is saved and carried on to the next move. This option allows players to save unused time and build up a buffer to be used when needed. For example in a game of Rummikub when a move may simply consist of picking up another tile all unused time is saved for use at a later stage when a player may want to spend more time to think about his move.

-Up count option: each player's clock records the total time a player is using for all his moves; each time a player's clock is faced upwards his clock will continue the up count.

-Move counter option: each time a player's clock is faced upwards his counter adds one move to his total number of moves."

Keep in mind the Dutch (?) auction game by C. T. Chew used in "Stop the Clock!"

Where to buy

Visit the Perfect Press' Island Shop and buy the boxed game, *Tets*. Or, you can go online and download the PDF files for the *Tets*, cut them out and assemble them for yourself. The prize cards inside the *Tets* you can download and print on a 3-D printer.

Awaiting further development

Does this make sense? "If the player adds a card to a row, nothing else happens in the turn, and the next player goes into action."

Does this make sense? "Because each row holds a maximum of three cards, individual rows fill up pretty quickly."

Does this make sense? "You must pay close attention to the colors each player has in his or her pile before tossing a card into a row.

Does this make sense? "Otherwise, you might create a row with only the colors that another player wants for his or her collection!

Does this make sense? "After taking a row, the player adds the cards from that row into the color piles in front of her, and then sits out the rest of the turn.

Does this make sense? "After all the rows get taken, players create new rows and the process begins anew.

Does this make sense? "Play continues until someone pulls the end-of-round marker from the top of the draw deck, at which point everybody takes one of the current rows, and the game is over.

Does this make sense? "You never know what quadrant might come off the deck next, so luck plays a solid part in this game. But Tets still features plenty of strategic potential. You need lots of tiles to score the biggest points, however, strategically you need to make an if-then decisions.

Does this make sense? "Which strategy is best? Only time will tell—you have to play to know.

EarthSafe 2022

To play the game, it really helps to know the story, *Women Who Fell to Earth* and *Hunt for the Emeralda Treasure*. It is helpful to want to learn about printmaking, too. Most of all, it is mandatory to know the 1992 publication, *Earth's Scientists Warning to Humanity*, by the *Union of Concerned Scientists*. This little pamphlet started me on his journey to Emeralda Region and is always watching his back. How the situation is tied together is simple: Without the artists, scientists will likely fail in their mission to save Earth's human life sustainability.

Gates Prize Upgrade

No printmaking experience is complete without a Gates Prize upgrade—but beware of the Omnium Gatherum. He wants to smother all of us in CO^2. The motive of all Emeralda Games is to destroy the Ominium Gatherum and all that this shade stands for.

In the online version, played on the Web, it may be possible that you can interact with the person closest to you on the PrintWorld Map of the Earth. This person is a Proximate, i.e., you found them using their Kyber Etching press at almost the same time as you were using your Kyber Press.

Origin of "Tets"

Tets is based on *Easy Come, Easy Go*, a dice game for 2 to 8 players, costing about $12 and described in "Trading Card Games for Dummies," Page 305.

Back story: History of Emeralda Region and Perfect Press' Island's special place in the region

Starting in 1966 and continuing for nineteen years, I taught printmaking and media arts at the University of Washington. I explored every kind of printmaking, from traditional woodcuts to the beginnings of photography, video and computer graphics. I left the real university to find a better teaching and study environment where I could unleash his skills and Imagineering.

In 1992 I arrived at my imaginary place in my cyberspace and I named it, *Emeralda Region*, respecting the already established name for Seattle, the *Emeralda City*. I acknowledged, too, Frank Baum's name for the perfect city in the *Wizard of Oz*. I found the Holy Grail of experiencing the ever-changing world of teaching, researching and practicing the vast domain of the media arts. I found where these arts originated and I see where the path is leading.

The routine of an Emeralda Resident-in-Stay is daily visits to one of the ten islands in the order in which the islands are named, alphabetically. The first day you spend in ArtsPort; the second day, E'Studios and so on. The fifth day—today—you spend on Perfect Press.

Printmaking is the root of all modern technologies and the history of technology is sprinkled with chance occurrences and people meeting to work on shared ideas. On this island the culture is about printmaking and ways to make great fine art through learning total systems, i.e., from the handiwork of making personal presses suitable for printing playing-card sized etchings and other kinds of printing plates of the newest kind, the 3-D printed collagraphs.

On each of the ten islands in Emeralda Region, the culture differs from one compared to the next. However, all the communities are essentially "print-centric," which means that the cultural teaching, research and practices are based on the plain truth that all technologies today are descended from the simplest kind of printing. Perfect Press sits to one side of the middle of Emeralda, and Perfect Studios sits on the other side. They are a complementary pair.

The choice of the game, *Easy Come Easy Go* as a starting point for Tets was a choice I found was made arbitrarily because I used the book, *Trading Card Games for Dummies*, Part V, and the author offered up a series of ten easy games to help think about card game basics of some TCGs. The number ten fits nicely with the ten-island campaign to discover ATC/TCG of Emeralda.

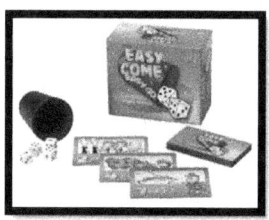 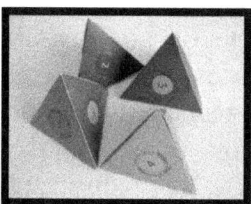

"Easy Come Easy Go" game components, costing about $12. See if you can create the designs for "Tets" similarly.

The promotional copy, above, was drawn from my novel, *Rembrandt's Ghost in the New Machine* as one of my games' back stories. As with the other games suggested in this collection, a back story helps to tie the printmaking theme common to Emeralda Trading Card Games.

The back story for Tets is related to my actual experience told earlier—how I was typing on an Apple II+ computer in 1979, and words seem to appear on their own on the screen. With artistic intuition, I decided I was being dictated to by an alien woman, better known as a "muse" in typical accounts of creativity in art, music, theater, literature, etc.

The story gets more complicated as it seemed there was more than one muse, and each ones' influence was contradictory to the others. I decided to name these muses, settling on the number 4 to go with his stories about his fictional, *Women Who Fell to Earth."* His favorite is Media, the inspiration for all media art and inventor of printmaking. Tetra I call the mysterious one, full of mystery and unfathomable wisdom. Techne is the engineer and Aural is the blind one famous for her singing, poetry and story-telling skills.

Their colors are, respectively, Green for Media, Yellow for Aural, blue for Tetra, and Red for Techne. Their stones are emerald, yellow beryl, aquamarine and morganite.

Conclusion to Chapter 5

Tets is the fifth of the games to be written down in a more-or-less cogent way—but allowing plenty of room for development by other people with more game skills. The method of play, above, I wrote on July 17, 2013, on the Domain-of-Expertise called "Perfect Press," which is for artists to share in teaching-and-learning, research, practice-and-production, and service to the printmaking world and all humanity.

The reader is invited to edit, tune and hack the text above until it is a better, real, workable game. It will be hard work, but it is fun and rewarding, this is a promise.

Chapter 6: Available

A Fantasy Printmaking and Real Estate Trading Card Game for 3 to 6 players. *Available* is a quick, fun game nominally about buying and selling island properties. During two phases, players first bid for several properties then, after all properties have been bought, sell them for the greatest profit. Based on the imaginary place, Emeralda, the game is set on the ten islands in Emeralda Region. It's a little bit like Monopoly, but simpler and faster. Each property has a building on it where historically famous printmaker had a printmaking studio. If you buy this available property, you get the studio and all the artifacts in it. Imagine what you might find! The cards have trivia, incidents and flash fiction encounters between the artists and their muses.

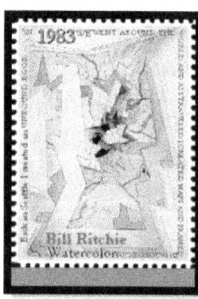 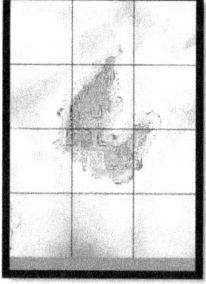

These two cards are placeholders. They would show what the deeds to properties in Emeralda look like, found in the Ritchie Family Collection of Ephemera.

The descriptive text for *Available* reads:

Available is a quick, fun game nominally about buying and selling real estate. During the game's two distinct phases, players first bid for several islands then, after all islands have been bought, sell the islands for the greatest profit.

Based on the imaginary place, Emeralda, the collectible trading card game, *Available*, is a fascinating real estate game based on the ten islands in Emeralda Region. It's a little bit like Monopoly, but it is a simpler and faster game.

The importance of ten

The ten islands idea, called *Domains of Expertise,* for this real-estate based game is based on an opinion that, for a well-rounded educational experience, a person needs ten skill sets. Each of the ten islands represents one of the skill sets. The imagined population residing on the island presents a culture dominated by representations of their particular skill.

The importance of forty

Each island has ten districts, denoted by a color code (see below). The Available property has a building on it of which it is known that a famous, historically famous printmaker once lived there. If you buy this available property, you get the house and everything in it—all the artifacts the artist left behind at their demise. Imagine what you might find!

Game properties

Available comes with a property deck of deed cards numbered 1 to 40, a deck of checks (with values between VOID and $54,000, and a bunch of money counters called "Emeralda Dollars," beautiful brass and copper-colored badge-like coins (and, in Collector sets, made of real metals). Some of the "dollars" are worth $1,000 and some are worth $2,000 and you can tell by the colors—copper for the former and brass for the latter.

Game mechanic

The goal of *Available* involves ending with the most money, both from the *Available* sector (including the house) sales, entire island sales and from any unspent capital left over from the start of the game. *Available* plays in two rounds: Round One is *Available* property purchase and, then, Round Two, the sale of the property. Both rounds use modified bidding systems, which give the game quite an interesting feel.

Sector colors in *Available*

The color codes of each sector of the islands emerged from the novels, when four women—sisters in a sextuplet—from "The Flower Planet," *Fleura*, come to Earth, each in her own module from the mother ship. Each of the alien women carries a souvenir stone from her planet—the forms of beryl we know as the precious gems, emerald, morganite, aquamarine and yellow beryl. Something about the stones describes the personality of each sister. These are their properties, or attributes.

The cards also have trivia, such as the incidents encountered by the sisters with the famous artists—all fictional, of course.

There is an ongoing connection with printmaking and the kind of trivia, technique and historic facts that make up the culture on these islands in Emeralda Region.

Starting play

In Round One, players bid on the right to pick one of this turn's available properties' deeds that are laid out in the center of the table—the number of players decides how many properties' deeds will be laid out. So, at the start of each turn, the dealer draws one deed card for each player and places these deed cards face up in the middle of the table.

Rather than bid on specific available properties' deeds, the players bid for the right, or option, to take and hold for later sale the property with the highest number. Bidding goes around the table, and if your bid is highest, you get the available property.

For example, you put three of your $1,000, Emeralda coins (the copper ones) by the property with the highest value showing on its deed. You've bid $3,000 Emeralda Dollars. If that is the highest bid, you get the highest numbered deed card—the available property in that round—in the auction—plus you get to be the next dealer.

Bidding

A lot of the game's fascination comes from the delightful contortions of the bidding system. In Available, only the player with the highest bid each turn spends the full amount of money—emptying his or her credit line of available investment capital. Everybody else after the player with the highest bid, in descending order of what their bid is either pays only half (rounded up to the nearest amount) of what they bid or gets a property for free.

In some instances (and this is very rare indeed) the bidding goes to the Stop The Clock mode, the Action, not an auction, but a timer which tests peoples' ability to resist bidding until the clock ticks down, down, down on the price until someone shouts, "Stop the Clock!"

(Credit goes to C. T. Chew, for whom all rights are reserved.) What makes this happen is a secret.

To make your bid you place one or more of your coins in front of you. The player around the circle, moving to the left, either bids more coins than you or passes by and takes the lowest valued available property.

If, on the other hand, the next player after you bids higher, then play continues to the next person around the table. If she passes after bidding, then she gives half of her bid (rounded up to the next higher amount) to the bank, pulls the remainder back into her stockpile, and takes the lowest valued property deed card that is still up for grabs.

After all of the other players drop out of the bidding, the last bidder puts his entire bid into the bank before taking the highest numbered deed card available that turn. Round One continues until all the properties' deed cards get sold. After they are all gone, play shifts to Round Two, in which the players sell the properties that they bought for as much money as they can.

Secret process

Here, the bid mechanism turns secret. A player flips up one card for each player from the Check Deck t show its value. This is a special check from the Emeralda Bank Checking account good for purchasing Available property. Now, players each secretly select a card from their stack of properties that they bought in Round One and place this face down in front of them.

All players then turn over their property deed cards at the same time. The player with the highest property number takes the highest Check in the set, and so on, down to the person with the lowest-numbered property sitting before them.

What happens

Sometimes you get a really good property with a small amount deed card simply because a bunch of high-value checks popped out in that round and everyone else had actually lower-value properties than you.

Or, other things happen that require some clever thinking and gambling. For example, sometimes the checks that are turned up consist of a VOID check, a couple with small dollar amounts, and one really huge amount. You obviously want the biggest check, but how would you play it?

Would you play big, hoping to score the big check?

Do you get sly and play the middle-of-the-road card?

What if your opponents anticipate that you will go big, so they go really, really low, getting rid of their weak cards without worry or fear?

To win

In order to win the game—by having the highest total value of checks at the end of the game—you are presented with many important decisions to make!

Visit the Perfect Studios' Island Shop and buy the boxed game. Or, you can go online and download the PDF files for the *Available*, cut them out and assemble them for yourself. You can download and print on a 3-D printer the DIY printing plates for the prize cards inside the *Available* and print them on your Emeralda press.

Awaiting further development:
On EarthSafe 2022

To play the game, it is essential to know the back stories about Emeralda Region, how *Women Who Fell to Earth* and the life story of Elmer Gates, whose face is on the Emeralda Dollars. It is helpful to want to learn about printmaking, too, as well as printmaking history.

Most of all, it is mandatory to know the 1992 publication, *Earth's Scientists Warning to Humanity*, by the *Union of Concerned Scientists*. This little pamphlet started me on my journey to Emeralda Region and the UCS is always watching my back. How the situation is tied together is simple: Without the artists, scientists will likely fail in their mission to save Earth's human life sustainability.

You must try to tell this to the scientists; you might be surprised how they agree with you.

Gates Prize Upgrade

No printmaking experience is complete without a Gates Prize upgrade; but beware of the Omnium Gatherum. He wants to smother all of us in CO^2. The motive of all Emeralda Games is to destroy the Ominium Gatherum and all that this shade stands for.

In the online version, played on the Web, it may be possible that you can interact with the person closest to you on the PrintWorld Map of the Earth. This person is a Proximate, i.e., you found them using their Kyber Etching press at almost the same time as you were using your Kyber Press.[2]

---

[2] Kyber press is proposed to replace Halfwood in a gamer edition.

Origin of "*Available*"

Available is based on *For Sale*, a real estate game for 3 to 6 players, costing about $12 and described in the book, "Trading Card Games for Dummies," Pp 306-308.

Back story: History of Emeralda Region and Perfect Press' Island's special place in it

Starting in 1966 and continuing for nineteen years, I taught printmaking and media arts at the University of Washington. With his students I explored every kind of printmaking, from traditional woodcuts to the beginnings of photography, video and computer graphics. I left the real university to find a better teaching and study environment where I could unleash my skills and Imagineering. I aimed to be an online printmaking teacher.

In 1992 I arrived at my imaginary place in my cyberspace and I named it, *Emeralda Region*, respecting the already established marketing name for Seattle, the *Emeralda City*. I acknowledged, too, Frank Baum's perfect city in the *Wizard of Oz*. From my research on teaching hospitals dating back to 1776, I cobbled together new principles for a school and of experiencing the ever-changing world of teaching, researching and practicing the vast domain of the media arts.

I found that where these arts originated I could see where the path is leading, and in the role of an Emeralda *Resident-in-Stay* I daily visit one of the ten islands in the order in which the islands are alphabetically named. The first day you spend in ArtsPort; the second day, E'Studios and so on. By the sixth day—today—the voyager is on Perfect Studios.

On this island the culture is about asset management, legacy transfer and total systems. Alongside benches for making personal presses and printing plates, plans are laid out to ensure that what artists accomplish is not lost, but can be counted on being good and valuable to their life's goal, i.e., doing good to preserve Earth's human life sustainability.

While the cultures of each of the ten islands in Emeralda Region differ, all the communities are essentially "print-centric," which means that the cultural teaching, research and practices are based on the plain truth that all technologies today are descended from the simplest kind of printing. Perfect Studios sits alongside Perfect Press and, after it, the think tank called Ritchie's Institute for the Study of Multimedia Arts (RIISMA) on the other side.

The choice of the game, *For Sale* as a starting point for *Available* was a choice I found was made arbitrarily because I used the book, *Trading Card Games for Dummies*, Part V, and the author of this book offered ten easy games to help me (who is no card player) help think about card game basics of some TCGs. The number ten fits nicely with the ten-island campaign to discover ATC/TCG of Emeralda.

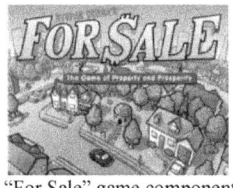 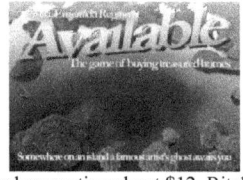

"For Sale" game components box costing about $12. Ritchie tried to create the designs for "Available" similarly at the right.

Some of the promotional copy, above, was taken from my unfinished trilogy, *Perfect Studios,* which I started writing—and living as I wrote them—in in the late 1980s. As with the other games suggested in this collection, a back story helps to tie the printmaking theme common to Emeralda Trading Card Games. The series evolved to include *Escape Emeralda,* a hidden object game conceived in 2009 and still under development.

Available is related to my actual experience described in earlier sections—how I was typing on an Apple II+ computer in 1979, and words seemed to appear on the screen on their own. I decided I was being dictated to by an alien woman, a "muse" and ever since I have gone along with it as her loyal servant in the real world. She's my boss.

The story gets more complicated as it seemed there was more than one muse, and each ones' influence was contradictory. I decided to name these muses, settling on the number 4 to go with his stories about his fictional, *Women Who Fell to Earth."* My favorite, I confess, is Media, the inspiration for all media art and inventor of printmaking. Tetra I calls the mysterious one, full of mystery and unfathomable wisdom. Techne is the engineer and Aural is the blind one famous for her singing, poetry and story-telling skills.

Their colors are, respectively, Green for Media, Yellow for Aural, blue for Tetra, and Red for Techne. Their stones are emerald, yellow beryl, aquamarine and morganite. These colors are applied to the four districts on the island wherein the properties are located.

Conclusion to Chapter 6

Available is the sixth of the games I wrote down in a more-or-less coherent and believable fashion—but allowing plenty of room for development by other people with real gaming skills. I wrote the method of play, above, on July 18, 2013, on the Domain-of-Expertise called "Perfect Press," which is for artists to share knowledge of artist's assets and legacy transfer, especially in the printmaking world.

The reader is invited to edit, tune and hack the text above until it is a better, real, workable game. It will be hard work, but it is fun and rewarding.

Chapter 7: FluxIP

A Fantasy Printmaking and Think Tank Trading Card Game for 2 to 6 players. FluxIP is a fun, quick, addictive card game that never plays the same way twice. The rules change as the game progresses, offering uniquely high replay value. Based on the imaginary place, Emeralda, this collectible trading card game is a fascinating Intellectual Property (IP) game. There are ten thematic decks based on the ten islands in Emeralda Region and is based on multimedia arts and got its name from the *Fluxus* movement of the last century. FluxIP comes with an IP deck of certificate cards with random catalog numbers and the worth of the item printed on them. The winning condition, or state, or goal, of the game is in the deck as well—and it can change just like the rules change!

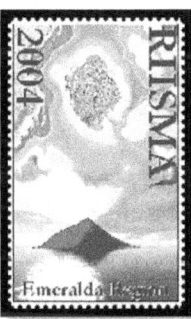 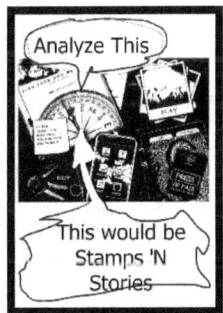

These two cards are placeholders. They would show what the certificates for properties in FluxIP look like and they are found in the Ritchie Family Collection used to finance Emeralda: The new school of printmaking.

The descriptive text for FluxIP reads:

FluxIP is a fun, quick, addictive card game that never plays the same way twice. The rules change as the game progresses, offering uniquely high replay value. Themes vary. For example, taking the Fluxx Pirates model, the promotion says that some cards let you play out of turn to take your enemies by surprise. This might be adapted to RIISMA's FluxIP by saying: Playing the Omnium Gatherum card gives you certain privileges but watch out for Exploiters amongst the team.

Based on the imaginary place, Emeralda, the collectible trading card game, FluxIP, is a fascinating Intellectual Property game. There are ten thematic decks based on the ten islands in Emeralda Region. It's a little bit like the consumer game line called Fluxx. FluxIP and is based on multimedia arts and got its name from the *Fluxus* movement of the last century.

The importance of ten

The ten islands idea, called Domains of Expertise, for this Intellectual Property based game is based on my opinion that, for a well-rounded educational multimedia experience, a person needs ten skill sets. Each of the ten islands represents one of the skill sets. The imagined population residing on the island presents a culture dominated by representations of their particular skill.

The importance of forty

Each island has ten districts, denoted by a color code (see below). The FluxIP property has a building on it of which it is known to be a repository for prints and related items to a certain printing technique. If you enter this FluxIP Museum, you get the rights to something in it—the artifacts or Intellectual Property—the IP in the name of the game.

Game properties

FluxIP comes with an IP deck of certificates cards with random catalog numbers and the worth of the item printed on them. A new type of stock certificate called ArtistsRIPStock is another possibility.

Game mechanic

The goal of FluxIP involves ending with the most cards and totaling the highest face value.

Sector colors in FluxIP

The color codes of each sector of the islands emerged from the printing techniques used in fine art printmaking. These are intaglio (red), relief (blue), yellow (planographic), and green (stencil). Something about the techniques makes the artwork distinctive in most cases, and sometimes it can be confusing and misleading.

Each technique says something about the history of the technique, the economies of the time the technique was flourishing, and the artists' situations when they employed them. These are properties, or attributes, of the art, and determine their Intellectual Property value.

The cards also have trivia, such as the incidents encountered by the artist and, in the case of some productions, the team of people who worked on the project. These are simply referred to as "stories." As with all Emeralda Games, there is an ongoing connection with printmaking and the kind of trivia, technique and historic facts that make up the culture on these islands in Emeralda Region.

Starting play of Round One

Every game play starts with the same basic rules: Draw a card and play a card on your turn, keep as many cards in your hand as you want, and (most importantly) when the game begins there is no way to win!

The winning condition, or state, or goal, of the game is in the deck as well—and it can change just like the rules change!

On your turn, you might play a new rule that overrides any of the basic rules, helps you complete a goal, or that does something completely different, such as forcing everyone to pass their cards to the left.

Also, you might play Keeper or Goal cards during your turn.

To win in the game of FluxIP, you need the right KEEPER cards in play (with names like Chocolate, Love, Money and Moon) to fulfill the current GOAL card.

Each GOAL specifies which KEEPER cards trigger it, i.e., bring it into effect or "realize" it.

In fact, every card in the deck tells you exactly how to play itself, making this one of the easiest games in Emeralda Region to teach to other people.

Round One

> In Round One, called Pre-production, players bid on the right to pick one of this turn's FluxIP properties' deeds that are laid out in the center of the table—the number of players decides how many properties' deeds will be laid out. So, at the start of each turn, the dealer draws one deed card for each player and places these deed cards face up in the middle of the table.

Starting play of Round Two

In Round Two, Production

Starting play of Round Three

In Round Three

Starting play of Round Four

In Round Four, called Post Production

Awaiting further development

The following is in boxes to indicate that it is copied verbatim from the original text describing Fluxx, the inspiration for this game and must be re-written or deleted or risk copyright infringement action.

Rather than bid on specific FluxIP properties' deeds, the players bid for the right, or option, to take and hold for later sale the property with the highest number. Bidding goes around the table, and if your bid is highest, you get the FluxIP property.
For example, you put three of your $1,000, Emeralda coins (the copper ones) by the property with the highest value showing on its deed. You've bid $3,000 Emeralda Dollars. If that is the highest bid, you get the highest numbered deed card—the FluxIP property in that round—In Round Four, called Post Production
A lot of the game's fascination comes from the delightful contortions of the bidding system. In FluxIP, only the player with the highest bid each turn spends the full amount of money—emptying his or her credit line of FluxIP investment capital. Everybody else after the player with the highest bid, in descending order of what their bid is either pays only half (rounded up to the nearest amount) of what they bid or gets a property for free.
In some instances (and this is very rare indeed) the bidding goes to the Stop The Clock mode, the Action, not an auction, but a timer which tests peoples' ability to resist bidding until the clock ticks down, down, down on the price until someone shouts, "Stop the Clock!" (Credit goes to C. T. Chew, for whom all rights are reserved.) What makes this happen is a secret.
To make your bid, you palace one or more of your coins in front of you. The player around the circle, moving to the left, either bids more coins than you or passes by and takes the lowest valued FluxIP property.
If, on the other hand, the next player after you bids higher, then play continues to the next person around the table. If she passes after bidding, then she gives half of her bid (rounded up to the next higher amount) to the bank, pulls the remainder back into her stockpile, and takes the lowest valued property deed card that is still up for grabs.
After all of the other players drop out of the bidding, the last bidder puts his entire bid into the bank before taking the highest numbered deed card FluxIP that turn.
Round One continues until all the properties' deed cards get sold. After they are all gone, play shifts to Round Two, in which the players sell the properties that they bought for as much money as they can.

Secret process

Here, the bid mechanism turns secret. A player flips up one card for each player from the Check Deck t show its value. This is a special check from the Emeralda Bank Checking account good for purchasing FluxIP property. Now, players each secretly select a card from their stack of properties that they bought in Round One and place this face down in front of them.

All players then turn over their property deed cards at the same time. The player with the highest property number takes the highest Check in the set, and so on, down to the person with the lowest-numbered property sitting before them.

What happens

Sometimes you get a really good property with a small amount deed card simply because a bunch of high-value checks popped out in that round and everyone else had actually lower-value properties than you.

Or, other things happen that require some clever thinking and gambling. For example, sometimes the checks that are turned up consist of a VOID check, a couple with small dollar amounts, and one really huge amount. You obviously want the biggest check, but how would you play it?

Would you play big, hoping to score the big check?

Do you get sly and play the middle-of-the-road card?

What if your opponents anticipate that you will go big, so they go really, really low, getting rid of their weak cards without worry or fear?

To win

In order to win the game—by having the highest total value of checks at the end of the game—you are presented with many important decisions to make!

Visit the Perfect Studios' Island Shop and buy the boxed game. Or, you can go online and download the PDF files for the FluxIP, cut them out and assemble them for yourself. You can download and print on a 3-D printer the DIY printing plates for the prize cards inside the FluxIP and print them on your Emeralda press.

Awaiting further development:
On EarthSafe 2022

To play the game, it really helps to know the back stories about my imaginary place, Emeralda Region, and my story of how *Women Who Fell to Earth;* also, the life story of Elmer Gates, whose face is on the Emeralda Dollar. It is helpful to want to learn about printmaking, too, as well as printmaking history.

Most of all, it is mandatory to know the 1992 publication, *Earth's Scientists Warning to Humanity, by the Union of Concerned Scientists*. This little pamphlet started me on my journey to Emeralda Region and the UCS is always watching my back. How the situation is tied together is simple: Without the artists, scientists will likely fail in their mission to save Earth's human life sustainability.

You must try to tell this to the scientists; you might be surprised how they agree with you.

Gates Prize Upgrade

No printmaking experience is complete without a Gates Prize upgrade—but beware of the Omnium Gatherum. He wants to smother all of us in CO_2. The motive of all Emeralda Games is to destroy the Ominium Gatherum and all that this shade stands for.

In the online version, played on the Web, it may be possible that you can interact with the person closest to you on the PrintWorld Map of the Earth. This person is a Proximate, i.e., you found them using their Kyber Etching press at almost the same time as you were using your Kyber Press.[3]

Origin of "FluxIP"

"FluxIP" is based on "Fluxx," a series of various card decks, costing about $12 and described briefly in "Trading Card Games for Dummies," Pages 308-309.

---

[3] Kyber press is a suggestion for renaming Halfwood for a gamer edition, where the press is part of playing the game.

Back story: History of Emeralda Region and RIISMA Island's special place in it

Starting in 1966 and teaching continuously for nineteen years, I was a printmaking professor instructing in all the media arts at the University of Washington. With my students I explored every kind of printmaking, from traditional woodcuts to the beginnings of photography, video and computer graphics. I left the brick-and-mortar university, dreaming of a better teaching and study environment where I could use my imagineering vision. I aimed to be an online printmaking teacher.

In 1992 I conceived an imaginary place in cyberspace and I named it, Emeralda Region, respecting the already established marketing name, Emeralda City for Seattle. I acknowledged Frank Baum's city in the *Wizard of Oz*. From my research on teaching hospitals that date back to the mid-eighteenth century, I cobbled together new principles for a school of printmaking in the ever-changing world of teaching, researching and practicing the vast domain of the media arts.

I found where the printing arts originated and I thought I could see where the printmaking pathwasy was leading. In playing the role of an Emeralda Resident-in-Stay, I mindfully visit one of the ten islands in the order in which the islands are named, alphabetically. The first day I spend on ArtsPort; the second day, E'Studios and so on. By the seventh day—today—I'm on the think tank island called Ritchie's Institute for the Study of Multimedia Arts (RIISMA).

On this island the culture is about total systematic research, digging deeply into the past and casting grappling hooks into the future of the media arts and the people who use them. It's a place populated by people using their hands and their minds while they learn at workbenches how to make personal presses and printing plates.

Also they study plans that might ensure that what they accomplish is not lost, but can be counted on being good and valuable, i.e., Intellectual Property (IP) as well as physical property.

While the culture of each of the ten islands in Emeralda Region differ from each other, all the communities are "print-centric," which means that the cultural teaching, research and practices are based on the plain truth that all technologies today are descended from the simplest kind of printing. RIISMA sits alongside Perfect Studios and, after it, SPEACON on the other side.

The choice of the game, Fluxx as a starting point for FluxIP was a choice Bill found was made arbitrarily because I used the book, *Trading Card Games for Dummies*, Part V, and its authors offered ten easy games to help me (who is no card player) think about card game basics of TCGs. The number ten I made up to fit with the ten-island campaign to discover ATC/TCG of Emeralda. Fluxx sells varietal themes—Pirates, Family, Oz, Eco, etc.

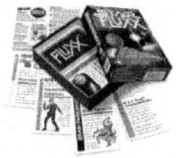 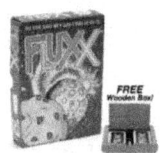 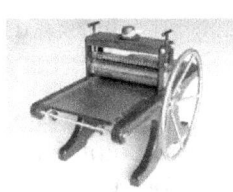

> "Fluxx" game components box costing about $12. Ritchie tried to re-create the designs for "FluxIP" similarly to include the Kyber press, right.

Some of the editorial copy, above, was taken from my unfinished trilogy, *Perfect Studios*, which I started writing in the late 1980s. As with the other games suggested in this collection, a back story helps to tie the printmaking theme common to Emeralda Trading Card Games. The series evolved to include Escape Emeralda, a hidden object game conceived in 2009 and is still under development. Another resource is a screenplay, *Swipe* and an outline for a ten-volume graphic novel, *Printmaking Camp*.

The birth of FluxIP is related to my actual experience—how I was typing on an Apple II+ computer in 1979, and words seemed to appear on the screen on their own. I decided I was being dictated to by an alien woman, a "muse" and ever since I have gone along with it as her loyal servant in the real world.

The story gets more complicated as it seemed there was more than one muse, and each ones' influence was contradictory to the others. I decided to name these muses, settling on the number 4 to go with his stories about my short story, *Women Who Fell to Earth*.

My favorite is Media, the inspiration for all media art and inventor of printmaking. Tetra I call the mysterious one, full of mystery and unfathomable wisdom. Techne is the engineer and Aural is the blind one famous for her singing, poetry and story-telling skills.

Their colors are, respectively, Green for Media, Yellow for Aural, blue for Tetra, and Red for Techne. Their stones are emerald, yellow beryl, aquamarine and morganite. These colors are applied to the four depositories on each island wherein the Intellectual Properties are located.

Conclusion to Chapter 7

FluxIP is the seventh of the games to be written down in a more-or-less coherent and believable fashion—but allowing plenty of room for development by other people with real gaming skills. The method of play, above, was written on July 19, 2013, on the Domain-of-Expertise called "RIISMA," which is for artists to do "think tank" kinds of research and share knowledge related to the multimedia arts in the printmaking world.

The reader is invited to edit, tune and hack the text above until it is a better, real, workable game. It will be hard work, but it is fun and rewarding.

Chapter 8: LightsOut

A Public Speaking and Fantasy Printmaking Trading Card Game for 2 to 4 players. LightsOut and is based on talking about various aspects of multimedia arts and is a humorous way to combat stage fright people suffer and, opposite this, to silence windy people who have love talking too much. Ten cards, numbered one to ten, are dealt to each player. The number on the card—corresponding to the alphabetical order of the names of the islands they represent—represents the card's relative power of light or dark, but also for the order that the card do their thing during the scoring phase. It is played with islands with powers of darkness and locks to deflect other islands' attempt to douse the lights and end the speech. The two biggest islands in the region look formidable and they can douse the lights better than any of the others.

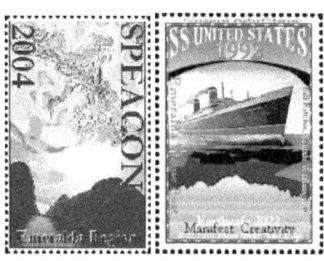

These two cards are placeholders. They would show what the certificates for properties in LightsOut look like and they are found in the Ritchie Family Collection used to finance Emeralda: The new school of printmaking.

The descriptive text for LightsOut reads:

LightsOut is a fun card game that offers unique lessons. Themes vary. For example, taking the Light Speed (a tabletop battleship game) model, the promotion says that some cards let you play out of turn to blow away your fear of public speaking by surprise. A sea war is adapted to SPEACON's LightsOut.

Based on the imaginary place, Emeralda, LightsOut, is a fascinating game of speaking, consulting and design. It's a little bit like the sea battle game called Light Speed. LightsOut and is based on talking about various aspects of multimedia arts and is a humorous way to combat stage fright many people suffer and, opposite this, to combat windy people who have a love for talking.

The importance of ten

The ten islands idea, called Domains of Expertise, for this public speaking-based game is based on an opinion that, for a well-rounded educational multimedia experience, a person needs ten skill sets. Each of the ten islands represents one of the skill sets. The imagined population residing on the island presents a culture dominated by representations of their particular skill.

Ten cards, numbered one to ten, are dealt to each player. The number on the card—corresponding to the alphabetical order of the names of the islands they represent—represents the card's relative power of light or dark, but also for the order that the card do their thing during the scoring phase.

Smaller islands can do their thing (up or down the lights) before the bigger islands. However, their degree of effectiveness is less so the lights don't go down as much.

Medium-sized islands get more than one try at the light switcher or they feature locks to deflect other islands' attempt to change the light level. The two biggest islands in the region look formidable and they can douse the lights better than any of the others.

Game mechanic

The goal of LightsOut involves ending with the most cards and totaling the highest face value. It uses a simultaneous play system. Each player gets a deck of ten islands, which the player shuffles a few times. When all the players look to be ready, someone counts down and says, "And now, here's our speaker!"

At that moment, everybody starts flipping over island cards and placing them on the table as fast as possible. This part of the game ends when the first person puts out her last island card and says, "Wait!"

The importance of forty

Each island has ten sectors, denoted by a color code (see below). The *LightsOut* sector denotes how close the card sits to the power switch.

Sector colors in LightsOut

The color codes of each sector of the islands emerged from the printing techniques used in fine art printmaking. These are intaglio (red), relief (blue), yellow (planographic), and green (stencil). Something about the techniques makes the artwork distinctive in most cases, and sometimes it can be confusing and misleading.

Each technique says something about the history of the technique, the economies of the time the technique was flourishing, and the artists' situations when they employed them. These are properties, or attributes, of the art, and determine their Public speaking value.

The cards also have trivia, such as the incidents encountered by the artist and, in the case of some productions, the team of people who worked on the project. These are simply referred to as "stories." As with all Emeralda Games, there is an ongoing connection with printmaking and the kind of trivia, technique and historic facts that make up the culture on these islands in Emeralda Region.

Starting play of Round One

(probably brought forward from previous game, FluxIP)

Round One

(probably brought forward from previous game, FluxIP)

Secret process

(brought forward from previous game, FluxIP)

What happens

(brought forward from previous game, FluxIP)

To win

(brought forward from previous game, FluxIP)

On EarthSafe 2022

To play the game, it really helps to know the back stories about Emeralda Region, how Women Who Fell to Earth and the life story of Elmer Gates, whose face is on the Emeralda Dollars. It is helpful to want to learn about printmaking, too, as well as printmaking history.

Most of all, it is mandatory to know the 1992 publication, Earth's Scientists Warning to Humanity, by the Union of Concerned Scientists. This little pamphlet started this games' developer, Bill Ritchie, on his journey to Emeralda Region and the UCS is always watching his back. How the situation is tied together is simple: Without the artists, scientists will likely fail in their mission to save Earth's human life sustainability.

You must try to tell this to the scientists; you might be surprised how they agree with you.

Gates Prize Upgrade

No printmaking experience is complete without a Gates Prize upgrade—but beware of the Omnium Gatherum. He wants to smother all of us in CO_2. The motive of all Emeralda Games is to destroy the Ominium Gatherum and all that this shade stands for.

In the online version, played on the Web, it may be possible that you can interact with the person closest to you on the PrintWorld Map of the Earth. This person is a Proximate, i.e., you found them using their Kyber Etching press at almost the same time as you were using your Kyber Press.

Origin of "LightsOut"

"LightsOut" is based on "Light Speed," costing about $12 and described briefly in "Trading Card Games for Dummies," Pages 309-310.

Back story: History of Emeralda Region and SPEACON Island's special place in it

Starting in 1966 and teaching continuously for nineteen years, I was a printmaking professor instructing in all the media arts at the University of Washington. With his students I explored every kind of printmaking, from traditional woodcuts to the beginnings of photography, video and computer graphics.

In 1985 I took permanent leave of the brick-and-mortar university—I resigned. I dreamed of a better teaching and study environment. Somewhere, out there, the thought was that I could use my imagineering vision to teach better, do better research, practice and be more productive and do good service to the community and country. Since 1980 I had a plan to be an online printmaking teacher and go on teaching after I was dead.

Years later I conceived an imaginary place in cyberspace and I named it, *Emeralda Region*. It is my printmaking teacher's heaven and was so named for Seattle, the "Emerald City," and the "Emerald Valley" of Western Oregon, and is reminiscent of Frank Baum's city in the *Wizard of Oz*.

A factory school of printmaking

Out of my discovery of the roots of teaching hospitals that date back to the mid-eighteenth century, I cobbled together new principles for a factory school of printmaking in the ever-changing world of teaching, researching and practicing the vast domain of the media arts.

I found where the printing arts originated and I see where the path is leading, and in the role of an Emeralda Resident-in-Stay I mindfully visit one of the ten islands in the order in which the islands are named, alphabetically. The first day I spend on ArtsPort; the second day, E'Studios and so on. By the eighth day—today—I am on the island called *Speaking, Consulting, Teaching and Instructional Design* (SPEACON).

On this island the culture is about excellence in all kinds of multimedia arts blended with face-to-face communication skills that facilitate learning. It's a place for people accustomed to using their hands and their minds toward guiding and enlightening others—young and old. They improve their communication skills while working at workbenches making personal presses and printing plates—the products of this factory school. Also they study being good and valuable through public speaking, consulting, teaching and instructional design of serious games.

The culture of each of the ten islands in Emeralda Region varies but all the communities are essentially "print-centric," which means that the cultural teaching, research and practices are based on the simple truth that all technologies today are descended from the simplest kind of printing. SPEACON sits alongside RIISMA and Video Island on the other side.

The choice of the game, *Light Speed* as a starting point for LightsOut was a choice I made arbitrarily because I used the book, *Trading Card Games for Dummies, Part V*, in which its author offered ten easy games to help (no card player) think about card game basics. The number 10 I fits the ten-islands campaign to discover ATC/TCG of Emeralda. Light Speed sells varietal themes, starting with outer space games.

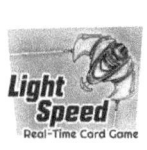
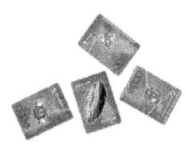
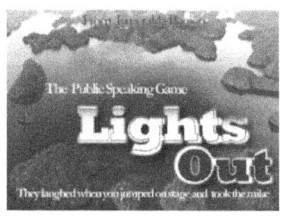

"Light Speed" game components box costing about $12. It is available as a down loadable PDF to make your own cards, fronts and backs. Ritchie tried to re-create the designs for "LightsOut" similarly to include the Kyber press, right.

Some of the editorial copy, above, was taken from my unfinished trilogy, *Perfect Studios*, which I began writing in the late 1980s. As with the other games suggested in this collection, a back story helps to tie the printmaking theme common to Emeralda Trading Card Games.

The series evolved to include Escape Emeralda, a hidden object game conceived in 2009 and still under development. Another resource is a screenplay, *Swipe*. Yet another is a ten-volume graphic novel, *Printmaking Camp*.

The birth of *LightsOut* is related to my actual experience I tell—how I was typing on an Apple II+ computer in 1979, and words seemed to appear on the screen on their own. I decided I was being dictated to by an alien woman, a "muse" and ever since I have gone along with it as her loyal servant in the real world. She is my boss, a personal dictator and represents the inspiration for all media art and invention of printmaking.

The story got to be more complicated as it seemed there was more than one muse, and each ones' influence was mildly contradictory to the others. I determined they numbered 4 and became the heart of his stories about the fictional, *Women Who Fell to Earth*.

I decided to name these muses, starting with my favorite muse, Media. Tetra I call the mysterious one, full of mystery and unfathomable wisdom. Techne is the engineer and Aural is the blind one famous for her singing, poetry and story-telling skills.

Their colors are, respectively, Green for Media, Yellow for Aural, blue for Tetra, and Red for Techne.

Their stones are emerald, yellow beryl, aquamarine and morganite. These colors are applied to the four depositories on each island wherein the Intellectual Properties are located.

Conclusion

LightsOut is the eighth of the games to be written down in a coherent fashion—but allowing plenty of room for development by other people with real gaming skills. The method of play, above, was written on July 20, 2013, on the Domain-of-Expertise called "SPEACON," which is for artists to do public speaking, consulting, teaching and instructional design and share knowledge related to the multimedia arts in the printmaking world.

The reader is invited to edit, tune and hack the text above until it is a better, real, workable game. It will be hard work, but it is fun and rewarding.

Chapter 9: Erase!

A Fantasy Printmaking and Video Art Trading Card Game for 2 to 4 players. *Erase!* is a fun, quick, addictive card game that offers uniquely high replay value. Themes vary according to available technologies. Some cards let you bulk erase your least-liked examples taken from the archives of pioneer video art tapes. Set in the imaginary place, Emeralda, *Erase!* is a game of restoring or destroying old-style video art. *Erase!* is based on looking at various selections of old video art tapes and is a humorous way to erase those you don't like and valorize the ones you do like. You get points by adding colored chips to your collection and by playing cards from your hand next to the appropriate chip stack. In order to win the game you are presented with many important decisions to make!

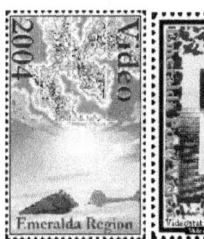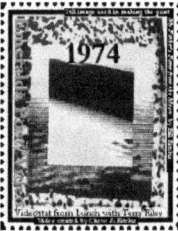

These two cards are placeholders. They would show what the cards for *Erase!* look like and they are found in the Ritchie Family Collection used to finance Emeralda, new school of printmaking.

The descriptive text for *Erase!* reads:

Erase! is a fun, quick, addictive card game that offers uniquely high replay value. Themes vary according to available technologies. For example, taking the Botswana (a card strategy game) model, the promotion says that some cards let you bulk erase your least-liked examples taken from the archives of pioneer video art tapes.

Set in the imaginary place, Emeralda, *Erase!* is a game of restoring or destroying old-style video art. *Erase!* and is based on looking at various selections of old video art tapes and is a humorous way to erase those you don't like and valorize the ones you do like.

The importance of six

Six cards, numbered zero to five, are dealt to each player. The number on the card—corresponding to the alphabetical order of the names of characters they represent—are the card's relative power of magnetism, but also for the order that the card do their *Erase!* thing during the scoring phase. Zero is the exception—it can be "Off" or "On" and thereby neutralized or high-powered respectively, depending on whether . . . (um, something else happens).

Game mechanic

To win this quick and challenging little game, you need the most points. You get points by adding colored chips to your collection and by playing cards from your hand next to the appropriate chip stack.

Each chip color has a corresponding set of six cards, numbered zero through five. A purple five, for example, goes next to the purple chip stack, making all those chips worth five points each. And they hold that value until the end of the game—unless, of course, someone covers up the five card with something lower, like a two, on, or the ever-popular zero card.

Smaller islands can erase tapes before the bigger islands. However, their degree of effectiveness is less so the tapes are not erased as much.

The importance of ten

The importance of forty

Sector colors in *Erase!*

To win

In order to win the game—by having the highest total value of points at the end of the game—you are presented with many important decisions to make!

Visit the Video Island Shop and buy the boxed game. Or, you can go online and download the PDF files for *Erase!*, cut them out and assemble them for yourself. You can download and print on a 3-D printer the DIY printing plates for the prize cards inside the *Erase!* and print them on your Emeralda press.

On EarthSafe 2022

To play the game, it really helps to know the back stories about Emeralda Region, how *Women Who Fell to Earth* and the life story of Elmer Gates (whose face is on the Emeralda badges). It is helpful to want to learn about printmaking, too, as well as printmaking history.

Most of all, it is mandatory to know the 1992 publication, *Earth's Scientists Warning to Humanity, by the Union of Concerned Scientists*. This little pamphlet started me on my journey to Emeralda Region and the UCS is always watching my back. How the situation is tied together is simple: Without true artists, scientists will likely fail in their mission to save Earth's human life sustainability.

You must try to tell this to the scientists; you might be surprised how they agree with you.

Gates Prize Upgrade

No printmaking experience is complete without a Gates Prize upgrade—but beware of the Omnium Gatherum. He wants to smother all of us in CO_2. The motive of all Emeralda Games is to destroy the Ominium Gatherum and all that this shade stands for.

In the online version, played on the Web, it may be possible that you can interact with the person closest to you on the PrintWorld Map of the Earth. This person is a *Proximate*, i.e., you found them using the Kyber Etching press[4] at almost the same time as you were using your Kyber Press.

Origin of "*Erase!*" by Bill Ritchie

"*Erase!*" is based on "Light Speed," costing about $12 and described briefly in "Trading Card Games for Dummies," Pages 309-310.

Back story: History of Emeralda Region and Video Island's special place in it

Starting in 1966 and teaching continuously for nineteen years, I was a printmaking professor instructing in all the media arts at the University of Washington. A turning point was his discovery of video art and its link to printmaking.

While I and my students explored every kind of printmaking, they also tried new media in photography, video and computer graphics.

---

[4] Kyber is a name suggested for a special edition of the Halfwood press.

In 1985 I took permanent leave of the brick-and-mortar university, dreaming of a teaching and study environment for multimedia. I knew I could use my imagineering vision to teach better, do better research, practice and be more productive and do good service to the community and country by freeing myself from academic constraints. I had started in 1980 to become an online printmaking teacher and hopes to go on teaching after I am dead.

To keep up with the times—for the 1980s were times when virtual reality was opening up new opportunities—I conceived of an imaginary place in cyberspace and I named it, *Emeralda Region*. It is my printmaking teacher's haven and I named my haven after Seattle, the "Emerald City," and the "Emerald Valley" of Western Oregon, and reminiscent of Frank Baum's Emerald City in the *Land of Oz*.

A factory school of printmaking

It was my research into the roots of the UW Hospital, known as a teaching hospital of the kind that dates back to the mid-eighteenth century, that made me cobble plans for a *factory school of printmaking*, my response to the ever-changing, vast domain of the multimedia arts.

I found it was in caves where the printing arts originated; I see where the evolutionary path of printmaking is leading, and in my self-appointed role of an *Emeralda Resident-in-Stay* I imagine what it would be like to visit the ten islands following the order in which the islands are alphabetically named.

Following this order, the first day is spent in ArtsPort; the second day, E'Studios and so on. By the ninth day—today—I am on the Emeralda Island called *Video*.

On this island the culture is about video production and island residents of Video comingle video production while they work at old-style workbenches for making personal presses and printing plates—the products of the Factory School of Cultural Arts Technologies. Also, they study at being good at the design and production of serious games like *Erase!*

The culture of each of the ten islands in Emeralda Region varies, but all the communities are essentially "print-centric," which means that the cultural teaching, research and practices are based on the plain truth that all technologies today are descended from the simplest kind of printing. Video sits between SPEACON and Video 'N Print Islands, each of which has its own culture and work style, yet related to Video because of their common ancestor—printmaking.

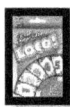

The choice of the game, *Botswana* as a starting point for *Erase!* is a choice I made arbitrarily because of the book I used as a guideline, *Trading Card Games for Dummies, Part V*, in which its author offered ten easy games to help people who are not card players to think about card game basics. Note that in the *Dummies* book, published a long time ago, Botswana was known in an earlier name, *Loco*. The number <u>six</u> is shoehorned in as I made it fit with the ten-island campaign to discover ATC/TCG of Emeralda.

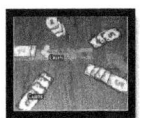 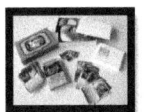 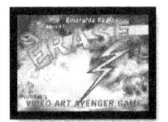 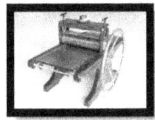

"Botswana" game was preceded by "Loco" and the components and box cost about $15. The game components for "*Erase!*" are in the memory of the press, downloadable as PDF files and as printable on 3-D printers. Second from the left is an array of mockups for "Video Dig Reloaded," another video game. The far right image suggests to re-create the designs for "*Erase!*" similarly and might include the Kyber press.

Birth of *Erase!*

The birth of *Erase!* is related to two actual events that happened to me in my early encounters with video and computer technologies. First, in 1979 I was typing on an Apple II+ computer, and words seemed to appear on the screen on their own.

I decided that I was being dictated to by an alien woman, a "muse," and ever since I have gone along with this notion as her loyal servant in the real world. I call her by the name, "Media." She is my personal dictator and represents the inspiration for all media art and inventor of printmaking.

The story got to be more complicated as it seemed there was more than one muse, and each one's influence was mildly contradictory to the others. I determined they numbered 4 and became the heart of his stories about the fictional, *Women Who Fell to Earth*.

I decided to name these muses, starting with my favorite, Media. "Tetra" I call the mysterious one, full of mystery and unfathomable wisdom. "Techne" is the engineer and "Aural" is the blind one who is famous for her singing, poetry and story-telling skills.

Their colors are, respectively, Emeralda Green for Media, Yellow for Aural, blue for Tetra, and Red for Techne. Their favorite stones are emerald, yellow beryl, aquamarine and morganite. These colors are applied to the four depositories on each island wherein their gems are hidden.

Toward the end of this phase of making up the features of Emeralda Region, I uncovered two male aliens were involved, too, and that all six—the four women and the two men—were sextuplets, all members of a family from *Fleura*, the Flower planet.

One of the men is the good guy; the other one is bad, because every story needs a villain. The bad guy, in this instance, has the power to bulk-erase magnetic tapes of video art in the Video Island Archives. In fact, his powers go much further than that!

The second experience I had that gave me the idea for this game was an experience with video. I was in the process of building a library of videos for teaching printmaking, and I was including the arts of papermaking, book arts, and the theories behind modern art.

A famous paper maker named Timothy Barrett came to give an all-day workshop at the UW, so I arranged to make a documentary video. It was going to be a first-rate video—one that Barrett could use in his promotion of Japanese papermaking in the USA.

Everything went well at the workshop. It was a long, hard day but the participants were greatly rewarded. When it was time to start editing the original tapes, I arrived at the video studio to begin to find that all but few minutes of the videos were mistakenly erased by one of the staff! Of the 400 minutes of recordings, all that was left was the closing five minutes.

Conclusion

Erase! is the ninth of the games I wrote down in a coherent fashion—but allows plenty of room for development by other people with more gaming skills than known to me. I wrote the method of play, above, on July 20, 2013. The reader is invited to edit, tune and hack the text above until it is a better, real, workable game. It will be a challenge, but it should be fun and rewarding.

Chapter 10: BAT

A Fantasy Printmaking Trading Card Game for 1 to 6 players. No matter how you think—random, serendipitous, linear—you can win a game of *BAT*. This is a game for thinking players, no matter whether it's linear or non-linear. The box includes a bunch of cards with one or more symbols on their faces. Look close and you notice that each card actually has five properties. Everybody plays at the same time in *BAT*. No time is lost waiting for someone else to take their turn. This keeps everyone involved all the time, which makes *BAT* a great game to play with groups of up to six players. Based on the French words, Bon A Tirer, it means a print is ready to publish. The winner is the person with the most cards in their pile and/or with the highest dollar value on the artwork.

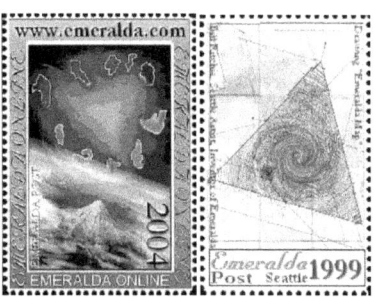

These two cards are placeholders. They would show what the cards for *BAT* look like and they are found in the Ritchie Family Collection used to finance Emeralda, new school of printmaking.

Linear or non-linear

Many people solve problems by progressing in a linear fashion, and if you are one of these people, then you automatically have trouble enjoying a game that makes you think in a flexible, random, make-it-up-as-you-go style. You probably feel frustrated playing a game like this, but that's the way it is.

BAT challenges that idea by adapting to your way of solving problems and seeing how to do something in order to make it right. You prefer a random approach? Fine. Want to do things in a linear, sequential order? That's fine, too. No matter how you think—random, serendipitous, linear—you can win a game of *BAT*. This is a game for thinking players, no matter whether it's linear or non-linear.

The descriptive text for *BAT* reads:

Set in the imaginary place, Emeralda, *BAT*, is a fascinating game of quick recognition and deduction and of restoring the creative process of printmaking—taking some of the leaps of imagination that brought printmaking into the realm of creative fine arts. The imaginary place is a region with a great lake, ten islands, and a pervasive multimedia arts culture. The year is 1984.

What's in the box

The box includes a bunch of cards with one or more symbols on their faces. Look a little closer and you notice that each card actually has five attributes, or properties.

1. A symbolic letter representing a printing process—"I" for intaglio, "R" for relief, "S" for stencil and "P" for planographic.

2. The number of the symbolic letters—one, two, three or all four of them.

3. The color of the symbolic letters—Red, green, yellow or blue.

4. The shading of the symbolic letters—outline only (in a colored outline) shaded (a 50% shade of the colored outline, same color tint) or solid, filled color.

5. A dollar value on the artwork represented on the card.

6. An open studio time card for working less than 3 hours is possible when holding the open studio card. (Text copied from a Singapore printmaking workshop).

Game mechanic

Everybody plays at the same time in *BAT*. No time is lost waiting for someone else to take their turn. This keeps everyone involved all the time, which makes *BAT* a great game to play with groups of up to six players.

To start the game, someone places twelve cards face-up in the middle of the table where everybody can see them. All players immediately begin looking for a set of three cards that match a very simple rule:

The three cards are either the same in one or more attributes (symbolic letter, the number of symbolic letters, their color, or one of the shading/outlining) or different in the remaining attributes.

For example, it might be the same symbol, "I," in red, with three of the "I" symbol, but the shading might be different.

Or, the set of three cards might be there are three cards with the same shading and the number of symbolic letters—like three of them on the face of the card—but the symbolic letter and their colors are different.

Or, you might find a group in which everything is different among three cards—nothing matches among them!

When a player thinks he or she sees a set like one of these, they call out *"BAT!"* Or, if they want to, *Bon A Tirer* in their best French possible. This temporarily pauses the play. They point out the three cards they spotted among the twelve cards on the table. They explain why the group follows the rules.

If everyone agrees that it is actually a set, that it matches the rule, the player adds those three cards to his or her Printer's Portfolio and then lays out three new cards in the emptied spaces. This starts the hunt for matching sets all over again—now with three new cards in place.

The winner is the person with the most cards in their pile and/or with the highest dollar value on the artwork.

The importance of twelve

I'm not sure why the inspiration for this game, "Set," uses 12 cards to start, but I'm not changing this until I'm sure it won't matter. Probably twelve is important because of the "set" being three and therefore divisible into twelve.

Probably, too, twelve is important because of the fact that there are three symbols in "Set"—the diamond, squiggle and oval. In *BAT*, there are four Letters (I,R,P,S), and four is also divisible into twelve, but the fact that in the mechanics of "Set" there are only 3 might throw off the mechanics. I wonder what would happen if the number were sixteen cards on the table?

Why sixteen? For one thing, sixteen times 4 equals 54, which is a good number and that's how many cards come in a deck of cards—fifty two cards and, most often, two jokers. All are divisible by 4.

The double importance of four

Already, above, I established that there are four printing process that are typical of the entire printing history and industry. This applies to the mechanical reproduction processes, but not always the photographic or electrographic processes, and has only a little to do with digital color on display screens. They belong in a different world of physics and electromagnetic fields.

For the purpose of game mechanic design, in the context of mechanical reproduction, we use I, R, P, and S which stand for *intaglio*, *relief*, *planographic* and *stencil*. We leave out photography and digital printing because we play *BAT* as a traditional printmaking game—not digital printmaking or photography, for example.

The second importance of four is that printmaking in color has typically been through the use of four separate colors—cyan, yellow, magenta and black (C,Y,M and K). Don't ask me why they use a K for black, they just do. You might also call these colors blue, yellow, red and black if "cyan" and "magenta" throw you off. If you are using paint, you might think about the primary colors as red, yellow and blue, plus white and black, which produce multitudes of colors but it gets a little confusing in actual practice because not all blue pigments are created equal, nor is any one of the other colors.

Starting play of Round One

Twelve cards are place in the center.

Round One

Play like you do "Set."

Starting play of Round Two

A catalog of prints is listed with the prices. Use these to tally the dollar value of your BATs.

Is there more?

If you want to make this an extensible game, you can tie it in with an auction game, as in *Available*, the Intellectual Properties game on Perfect Studios Isle (?). Or, since the game originated on Video N' Print isle—where all prints either come from video, or lead to video art—there could be a connection the another game yet, such as *Erase*, on Video Isle.

To win

In order to win the game you must have the highest total value of cards at the end of the game or the highest dollar value, and you may have both.

Buy now

Visit the Video 'N Print Island Shop and buy the boxed game. Or, you can go online and download the PDF files for the BAT, cut them out and assemble them for yourself. You can download and print on a 3-D printer the DIY printing plates for the prize cards inside the *BAT* and print them on your Emeralda press.

On EarthSafe 2022

To play the game, it really helps to know the back stories about Emeralda Region, how *Women Who Fell to*

Earth and the life story of Elmer Gates (whose face is on the Emeralda badges). It is helpful to want to learn about printmaking, too, as well as printmaking history.

Most of all, it is mandatory to know the 1992 publication, *Earth's Scientists Warning to Humanity*, by the Union of Concerned Scientists (UCS). This little pamphlet started me on my quest in the imaginary place, Emeralda Region. The UCS is always watching my back. How the situation is tied together is simple: Without engaging true artists in their mission, scientists will likely fail in their mission to save Earth's human life sustainability.

You must try to tell this to the scientists; you might be surprised how they agree with you. Think of Al Gore, whose slide show was a ho-hum affair for years. He had shown it and talked about climate change for a decade; when he finally got together with Hollywood-style designers and stylists, his show took off. He won an Academy Award. Not since he lost the presidential election had he got the attention of so many people.

Unfortunately, the momentum fell off, despite other big names in show business got behind film efforts to raise awareness. Who is to say, however, that it made no difference? We are waiting for the artists of the gaming media to put out a game to achieve mastery of any of the UCS five-points. Scientists and artists usually have a hard time communicating, the social and historic barriers are high, and the juggernaut of non-scientific, non-artistic production is so great.

Gates Prize Upgrade

No printmaking experience is complete without a Gates Prize upgrade—but beware of the Omnium

Gatherum. He wants to smother all of us in CO_2. The motive of all Emeralda Games is to destroy the Ominium Gatherum and all that this shade stands for.

In the online version, played on the Web, it may be possible that you can interact with the person closest to you on the PrintWorld Map of the Earth. This person is a Proximate, i.e., you found them using their Kyber Etching press at almost the same time as you were using your Kyber Press.

Origin of "BAT"

"BAT," this derivative, is copied over "Set," cost which costs about $12 and is described briefly in "Trading Card Games for Dummies," Pages 312-313.

Back story: History of Emeralda Region and Video Island's special place in it

(This section needs to be edited so as to reflect the importance of starting video art from printmaking.)

Also, the relationship of the illustrations on the cards—the prints—are open to creative solutions. For example, is there a connection between the "famous" artist or the "unknown artist" who authored the image and video and the connection video has to printmaking?

If former students of the UW printmaking program who were there when it all started are the featured illustrations, for example, that would be good. Look at Sato and Chew, Evans and others—some of whose work is still in the Graduated Students' folio.

A factory school of printmaking

Picture the working students' involvement in creating the game of BAT. They learn about printmaking at the same time they work on the mechanics and the parts of the game. This approach is called, "We build the road as we travel," a line taken from the famous Spanish co-operative, Mondragon.

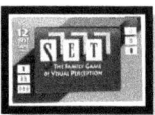 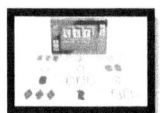 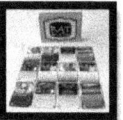 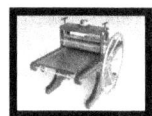

"Set" game's components and box cost about $15. Ritchie tried to re-create the designs for "BAT" similarly and might include the Kyber press. The game components for "BAT" are in the memory of the Kyber press, far right, downloadable as PDF files and as printable on 3-D printers.

The birth of *BAT*

The birth of *BAT* is related to an experience I had in 1979. I was typing on an Apple II+ computer when, weirdly, words seemed to appear on the screen on their own. I decided I was being dictated to by an alien woman, a "muse" and ever since I have gone along with it as her loyal servant in the real world. She is my boss and represents the inspiration for all media art and inventor of printmaking.

The story got to be more complicated as it seemed there was more than one muse, and each ones' influence was slightly contradictory. I determined they numbered 4 and became the heart of his stories about the fictional, *Women Who Fell to Earth*.

I decided to name these muses, starting with my favorite boss, Media. Tetra I call, "the mysterious one," full of mystery and unfathomable wisdom, her face always hidden. Techne is the "engineer" and Aural, the blind one, is famous for her singing, poetry and storytelling.

Their colors are, respectively, Green for Media, Yellow for Aural, blue for Tetra, and Red for Techne. Their stones are emerald, yellow beryl, aquamarine and morganite. These colors are applied to the four in printing.

Toward the end of this phase, I discovered two male aliens were involved, too, and that all six—the four women and the two men—are sisters and brothers—sextuplets, all members of a family from *Fleura*, the Flower planet. One man is the good guy; the other is the evil guy. Every story needs a villain, right? The bad guy, in this instance, has the power to bulk-*BAT* magnetic tapes of video art in the Video Island Archives.

Conclusion to Chapter 10

BAT is the tenth of the games I sketched in a coherent fashion—but allowing plenty of room for development by other people with real gaming skills. This method of play I wrote on July 22, 2013, on the Domain-of-Expertise called "Video 'N Print," which is for artists who produce video art related to prints, or prints related to video art.

The reader is invited to edit, tune and hack the text above until it is a better, real, workable game. It will be challenging work, but it is fun and rewarding.

Conclusion to Part II

Over two years have passed since I wrote the first drafts of these ten imaginary games that are based on real games, with no attempt to conceal my plagiarism. What has happened since?

For one thing, I decided to make my next ten year plan—2014-2023—the creation of the Northwest Print Center and Cultural Arts Business Incubator. The game division is part of the incubator and is print-centric in its culture. The game division is for games with purpose, which used to be called serious games.

Also during this time an Australian company opened a branch a few minutes' walk from our gallery called the Academy of Interactive Entertainment. Down the hall there is a Seattle Public High school which includes Game Design in its art classes.

Something compelled me to reopen this manuscript and see if I can tie in my plan to finance the NPC/CABI by selling my art as shares in the enterprise.

www.ingramcontent.com/pod-product-compliance
Lightning Source LLC
Chambersburg PA
CBHW052313220526
45472CB00001B/92